Advance Praise for *The Social Profit Handbook*

"Those of us in the business of creating social change all want to do great work, work that really moves our society forward. But figuring out just what success is and remaining committed to it turns out to be very hard. David Grant's great new handbook provides just the sort of wise counsel anchored by practical tools we need to help us get there. And, for me, his insistence that we truly take the time we need to get clear on what great work looks and feels like is a gift in itself."

—PHILLIP HENDERSON, president, Surdna Foundation

"David Grant's *Social Profit Handbook* is exactly what a handbook should be—accessible, enjoyable, practical, yet linked to important and thought-provoking theory. I have already applied his rubric assessment framework to my ongoing work as a consultant, as his examples are both refreshing and inspiring. Using his comforting educator's voice, Grant powerfully reframes perennial stumbling blocks into questions that can lead to responsible organizational approaches. I have spent my career attempting to improve the performance of foundations and nonprofits, and I genuinely see this resource as a breath of fresh air in the pursuit of effective implementation of strategy. This book will be a permanent resident on my 'foot-long bookshelf.'"

—NADYA K. SHMAVONIAN, former executive of
The Rockefeller Foundation and The Pew Charitable Trusts

"It has been my good fortune to help launch and run about a dozen mission-driven organizations over the past several decades. When I finished David Grant's wonderful new book, one thought eclipsed all others. Damn, I thought, I sure wish I had had this guide all those years! What a blessing that would have been!"

—JAMES GUSTAVE SPETH, author, *Angels by the River*;
founder, World Resources Institute;
cofounder, Natural Resources Defense Council

"Grant has the ability to take on incredibly big ideas, distilling them in a way that sustains their breadth and power, and bringing them into the civic sphere. In *The Social Profit Handbook*, Grant challenges disheartedness in our sector by providing a rational and aspirational context by which social profit can be better understood and pursued."
—CLEMENT A. PRICE, founding director of the Institute on Ethnicity, Culture, and the Modern Experience, Rutgers University

"Anyone in the business of improving lives—whether they spend their days in government or in mission-driven organizations—can benefit from this simple, elegant, and incisive guide to having not just *more* impact, but also the *right* impact. David Grant has produced a book that belongs on the shelves of every political and social leader interested in translating goals to successes."
—PETER WELCH, Congressman, US House of Representatives

"For many years, David Grant has helped our organization create firm foundations for new projects and initiatives through the principles outlined in this excellent roadmap for rethinking success. At last his guidance and wisdom are available to anyone fortunate enough to come across this book."
—ROBERT LYNCH, president and CEO, Americans for the Arts

"*The Social Profit Handbook* is the most meaningful, understandable, and practical guide to designing metrics that count in mission-driven work that I've ever read. What charity-rating organizations completely miss is what David Grant provides in this handbook—the means to measure what truly matters: impact. A must read for foundation leaders, nonprofit professionals, and even individual donors who want to understand the effect of their work, beyond the numbers."
—NINA STACK, president, Council of New Jersey Grantmakers

"I read *The Social Profit Handbook* over a weekend. My first day back in the office I recommended it to a new executive director and to one of my senior colleagues and referred to its core concept twice in my senior team meeting. Those of us who lead, oversee, and work in social-purpose organizations all know how setting out to describe a compelling vision and to hold ourselves accountable to reach it can be treacherous and disorienting. David Grant has written a timely and valuable guide that reminds us how important that journey is and describes how we can all build a map to navigate it with confidence."

—Antony Bugg-Levine, CEO, Nonprofit Finance Fund; founding board chair of the Global Impact Investing Network; former managing director of the Rockefeller Foundation

"Over many years of hosting grantee workshops led by David Grant, I have watched hundreds of individuals shift their mindsets before my very eyes. Executive directors and board members alike move from a palpable distaste and fear of assessment to a place where they embrace it as a major capacity-building tool. Like those workshops, *The Social Profit Handbook* gives every nonprofit or mission-driven business the tools they need to determine what 'success would look like' if they vigorously pursue what matters most to them. David's approach can help readers focus on mission and goals in entirely new ways."

—Wendy Liscow, program director, education and capacity building, Geraldine R. Dodge Foundation

"Wow. Who would have thought a book on assessment could be so compelling! If you are looking for a way to get your board and staff aligned and mobilized around a practical, impact-driven strategy, Grant's handbook is essential."

—George Hamilton, president and CEO of the Institute for Sustainable Communities

"Normally, when I hear the word *assessment*, I consider a nap. But *The Social Profit Handbook* is different. I enjoyed the jogging pace of the writing, the personal narrative, the linguistic memes for easy transmission. Even better, I'm already integrating David Grant's approach into existing assessment tools. Grant's fresh framework emphasizes formative feedback and rubrics to guide your team toward high performance. This is essential reading for mission-driven leaders dedicated to constantly improving their work."

—ADAM WERBACH, cofounder, Yerdle;
former president, Sierra Club

"This handbook is nothing less than revolutionary, and just what we need. If you can describe the change you most want to create, you can measure it, and others will come to value what you measure. Social profit, mission time, planning backwards: here's the answer to how we measure what matters most, focus our attention, and get to where we actually want to go as change-makers. David Grant is the most level-headed, poetic voice for how we might all live and perform closer to our own values. Three times now, his simple and provocative teaching has shifted the way I think and act, and through this book we can share his nuanced, accessible teaching with everyone. I will give this book to every social profit organization with which I collaborate."

—PETER FORBES, coauthor of *A Man Apart* and
cofounder of the Center for Whole Communities

THE
SOCIAL
PROFIT
HANDBOOK

The Essential Guide to Setting Goals,
Assessing Outcomes, and Achieving Success
for Mission-Driven Organizations

DAVID GRANT

Chelsea Green Publishing
White River Junction, Vermont

Editor: Joni Praded
Project Manager: Bill Bokermann
Copy Editor: Laura Jorstad
Proofreader: Helen Walden
Indexer: Margaret Holloway

Printed in the United States of America.
First printing March, 2015.
10 9 8 7 6 5 4 3 2 1   15 16 17 18

Our Commitment to Green Publishing
Chelsea Green sees publishing as a tool for cultural change and ecological stewardship. We strive to align our book manufacturing practices with our editorial mission
and to reduce the impact of our business enterprise in the environment. We print our
books and catalogs on chlorine-free recycled paper, using vegetable-based inks whenever possible. This book may cost slightly more because it was printed on paper that
contains recycled fiber, and we hope you'll agree that it's worth it. Chelsea Green is a
member of the Green Press Initiative (www.greenpressinitiative.org), a nonprofit coalition of publishers, manufacturers, and authors working to protect the world's endangered forests and conserve natural resources. *The Social Profit Handbook* was printed
on paper supplied by Thomson-Shore that contains 100% postconsumer recycled fiber.

Library of Congress Cataloging-in-Publication Data is available upon request.

Chelsea Green Publishing
85 North Main Street, Suite 120
White River Junction, VT 05001
(802) 295-6300
www.chelseagreen.com

For
Nancy, Ben, and Rob,
who are at the top of my
rubric on what matters,
and in memory of my dear friend
Clement Price,
who left social profit
in his wake

CONTENTS

FOREWORD

THERE'S A LINE IN THE MOVIE *Planes, Trains and Automobiles* that well describes the essence of David Grant's new book, *The Social Profit Handbook*. In this now classic film, Steve Martin turns to John Candy and says, "When you're telling your stories, here's an idea. Have a point. It makes it so much easier for the listener." And that's just what *The Social Profit Handbook* does for the nonprofit sector. It gives those of us in mission-oriented fields a better way to understand and communicate the point of our work.

Starting with the title, David introduces us to the term "social profit," a new and worthy addition to the nonprofit lexicon. He makes a compelling case that, in a society so heavily dependent on the work of nonprofits, we should have a better way to describe the point of our work. And that point is social profit. He argues that for too long our sector has been defined by what we are not ("not-for-profit") rather than what we are.

David's revised definition for the work and purpose of the sector is in itself a game-changer. If we get nothing more out of *The Social Profit Handbook* than this transformational definition, the book would be ground-breaking. But *The Social Profit Handbook* goes a step beyond to present yet another innovation for the sector, *rubrics*. David explains how for years rubrics have been used in the field of education, and then he skillfully translates this tried-and-true tool to the social profit sector. Indeed, it is

David's introduction of the *rubrics* approach to goal setting and assessment that forms the heart and soul of this book.

I first heard David present the use of rubrics for mission-driven organizations at a Robert Wood Johnson Foundation conference where he and I were both speaking. I'd done a good deal of work with the Geraldine R. Dodge Foundation during David's tenure as CEO, yet, until then, had never heard David's presentation on rubric-oriented assessment.

I listened, stunned by both the approachability and the practicality of his message. Here was a user-friendly way to think about assessment and evaluation, and a method I instinctively understood and about which I could actually get excited!

I will confess here that I have always been a bit intimidated by the world of evaluation. Early in my career someone chastised me for not knowing my "outputs from my outcomes," and that started my ambivalence toward the subject. And though traditional evaluation methods have since come a long way, the language of assessment and evaluation can still be off-putting and even sterile, especially when juxtaposed to the rich and vibrant work of the sector.

As I listened to David present the art of rubric creation, I saw a model in which those of us engaged in day-to-day social profit work could identify for ourselves, our stakeholders, and our beneficiaries what effective service delivery looks like. We could also use this model to set behavioral expectations from which to assess our own practice. Best yet, the principles involved with rubric creation encourage the definition of good, better, and best performance in areas we define as most important. Notice my use of the term *we* here. For that is another great part about rubric creation. We hold ourselves responsible for self-identifying essential areas of our work and how we will know we have done that work well. This is the essence of owning our work—and providing all those involved with self-generated standards for delivering that work with substance and pride.

From that day on, I nudged David to get this book written. I knew this would be a needed and necessary tool for those in the social profit sector who are looking for a better way to assess and measure the point of our work.

And now we have it. *The Social Profit Handbook* is written and promises to be a terrific resource for nonprofit executives, board members, and foundation officers.

Though most books on assessment, even those written from a qualitative approach, can be a little "heady" and academic in nature, this book comes from the heart as much as the head. David writes from his experience as a practitioner, and his voice strikes just the right tone. He writes with engagement, encouragement, and humor, much as you'd expect from a favorite teacher. It is clear how much he cares about the social profit sector and the success of mission-driven organizations.

At the end of the *Social Profit Handbook*, David mentions several books that he recommends for your "Foot-Long Book Shelf." One of those books is mine. *Nonprofit Lifecycles: Stage-Based Wisdom for Nonprofit Capacity*. I suggest to you that *The Social Profit Handbook* belongs on that same foot-long shelf. And while you're at it, I'd be proud to have you place our books side by side, since rubrics are to social impact as lifecycles are to nonprofit capacity.

I believe you will find David Grant's book, *The Social Profit Handbook*, to be a practical and user-friendly introduction to the world of rubrics and their ability to help articulate and measure the point of our work. For the field as a whole, *The Social Profit Handbook* also promises to make a seminal contribution, one I believe will stand the test of time.

And that's the point of a good book, isn't it?

Susan Kenny Stevens, PhD
Author, *Nonprofit Lifecycles*
November, 2014

ACKNOWLEDGMENTS

I OWE A GREAT DEBT TO GRANT WIGGINS for giving me the conceptual vocabulary to help people think differently about the purpose and practice of assessment.

Many friends and colleagues have encouraged me and made suggestions that have improved my manuscript. I would particularly like to thank those whose careful readings of my various drafts helped me shape the argument as a whole: Anne Barthel; Susan Stevens; Clement Price; Glenda Gilmore; Bob Weisbuch; Kevin Mattingly; Jack Kruse; and Steve Piersanti. My family members Nancy, Ben, Rob, and Jim similarly provided valuable counsel along the way.

I am deeply grateful to the Rockefeller Foundation for providing a writer's residency at The Bellagio Center in the fall of 2013, and to the staff and my fellow residents there for their support and inspiration.

Publisher Margo Baldwin, editor Joni Praded, and the whole team at Chelsea Green have been remarkable throughout the process that turns a rough manuscript into a finished book. They give new meaning to the phrase *adding value*.

I thank the social sector leaders in New Jersey who have participated in the Dodge Foundation's leadership series and the executive directors of the organizations I profile in the book. They have all been open-minded fellow learners—and my teachers as well.

Finally, when it comes to believing in the worth and vast potential of the social sector, I owe the most to those with whom I have worked side by side in mission-driven organizations: my colleagues at the Mountain School and the Geraldine R. Dodge Foundation.

INTRODUCTION

LEADERS OF MISSION-DRIVEN organizations know the benefits of having an "elevator speech"—a succinct explanation of why their programs and services exist. Authors should have their speeches ready, too, if they are asking for the attention of busy people. So let's imagine we have just entered an elevator on a fifth or sixth floor, heading down, and I manage to bring up the subject of my new book. Perhaps you say, "Good morning," and I say, "Guess what? I have a new book out." As we start to descend, you dutifully ask, "What's it about?"

I'd say, "It's about changing the way we think about assessment in what people call the social sector. I think the world's a mess, and I believe that the people who work in nonprofit organizations around the world—and the people who sit on their boards—can lead us out of it. I think they *will* lead us out of it. But they have to take a different approach to assessment first."

"Assessment," you mumble as the elevator opens into the lobby and you move for the door—quickly, I notice. I call after you, "I say we should stop even using the word *nonprofit*. We should call these organizations by what they *are* instead of by what they are not. We should call them *social profit* organizations."[1]

In my perfect world, you would turn back at this point, with considerably more interest, and repeat, "Social profit?"

"Yes," I would say as we walk through the lobby. "When you hear 'profit,' you think about money, right? We all do. That's because most investments, most activity, most decisions in the world are about creating or preserving *financial* profit.[2] But what we need is more *social* profit, from better schools to access to medical care, great art and music, clean rivers, high-functioning public transportation, and empowering young people to take care of themselves—anything that benefits people and their places and the planet we live on."

"But isn't social profit hard to measure?" you might ask.

"*Yes!*" I would exclaim. "That's why I am writing about assessment. We have to find an approach to defining social profit that gives us the incentives, the motivation, and the confidence to invest in it."

We would be at the street by now and ready to head our separate ways, but our brief metaphorical encounter has already unearthed the challenge that motivates this book and my proposed solution. We always know what our *financial* profit is because there is a basic unit of measure: a dollar, a rupee, a euro, a yuan. But we have to approach the reckoning of *social* profit in a different way. Social profit is about desired social benefits, and so it has to be defined locally depending on what a community of people values and what they need. It will never have a fixed or standard measure, and efforts to create one will get bogged down in endless quibbles and conflict about the measure itself. What we need are better *local* measures of both short-term and long-term social profit—and measures of a certain kind.

That's why I propose a different approach to assessment as a way forward. There are indeed metrics, numbers, that are important for measuring outcomes; we call that *quantitative* assessment, and we do it reasonably well. But to really and fully capture social profit—and, I would argue, to *create* the social profit you have in mind—you need *qualitative* assessment, too. You need to be able to measure things that can't be expressed in numbers. You need to bring people together around your best collective vision of what success looks like in the areas that matter most to you. That's what qualitative assessment does and that's what this book is about. In the pages ahead, I will show *how* to measure success in a way that helps you achieve it, illustrated by examples of organizations that have done exactly that.

I think we are all aware of a big problem—a world awash in financial profit, or at least the pursuit of it, when what it needs is social profit. Yet my approach to the problem involves a relatively small change in the way staffs and boards of social sector organizations—and the new breed of socially conscious businesses—define and assess their successes in creating social profit.

We might ask, with some justification, whether it should be governments that we primarily entrust with the creation of social profit. But with the exception of some cities that have managed to translate a vision of quality of life for all residents into public policies,[3] governments seem to be missing in action in this regard. Few people in the United States seem to expect our federal government to solve problems anymore, and my friends in other countries say the same about their national governments.

That is why I focus on the social sector, sometimes called the civic sector or the *third* sector, to differentiate it from government and business. Its whole reason for being is social profit. The sector is fragmented and cash-strapped, but collectively it can have enormous influence on the other sectors not only through its good work but also through its influence on voters and consumers. In short, I believe that social sector organizations can elevate the concept of social profit through the ways they define, pursue, and achieve the social benefits implicit in their missions. And after years of leading a grant-making foundation, and more years of consulting with organizations to strengthen their performance and measure their outcomes, I think I can help them do a better job.

Both the specific problems that social profit organizations address and the various benefits social profit organizations seek to bring about are substantial, even daunting. Yet I would like to focus on a smaller, more manageable problem. It is as if we are sitting in Pittsburgh and need to be in San Diego in a few days to give an important speech we have not yet written, and we have no travel plans. We know we have to write the speech, but let's do something we can manage first, like getting a plane ticket.

For me, the problem we can actually tackle is that organizations in the social sector, along with their funders, have not embraced the theory and practice of *formative* assessment—assessment practices whose primary purpose is to improve outcomes rather than judge them. They are far more likely to be familiar with *summative* assessment, which judges outcomes at the end. As assessment expert Paul Black explains, "When the cook tastes the soup, that's formative assessment. When the customer tastes the soup, that's summative assessment."[4] Most people in the social sector would not even consider the widespread lack of formative assessment a problem, because they have not paused long enough to think about it and learn how to do it. But I believe that if we can make progress with formative assessment, we can make progress on the measurement dilemmas inherent in the nature of social profit and, most important, we can do a better job of producing social profit.

Compared with the changes in the world that social profit organizations seek to bring about, embracing a new approach to assessment seems modest. But as any artist or designer knows, a small change—a few brushstrokes, a larger window in a dark room—can make a big difference. The organizations portrayed in the chapters that follow all faced particular challenges—both in measuring their performance for funders, and in improving their programs' effectiveness. The groups profiled range from large, national nonprofits to small, regional ones, and the obstacles they sought to address vary widely. But in most cases the eminently manageable changes and experimentation this book describes had a profound influence on their organizational cultures and their effectiveness in the areas that mattered most to them. My goal in this book is to help you—whether you are a board member, grantor, employee, or otherwise affiliated with a social profit organization—understand how the process works so that you can help your organization make the world a better place.

Here's what you can expect:

- Chapter 1 presents my central argument more formally and puts it into context for the book's various types of readers.
- Chapters 2 through 4 will explore the ways we think about three key concepts: the challenges (and dangers) inherent in measuring social profit; the purpose and practice of assessment; and the ways staffs and boards of social profit organizations spend time together.
- Chapter 5 introduces the *rubric*, a qualitative assessment tool that teachers all over the world use to help students be clear about criteria for success and get better at what they do.
- Chapter 6 offers some coaching to those who are designing rubrics for their own social profit work.
- Chapters 7 through 9 present examples of organizations (and groups of organizations) that have used rubrics to improve their effectiveness and create social profit.
- Chapter 10 confronts the difficulties of organizational change and provides some further coaching on how to overcome them.
- The afterword returns to the larger sense of purpose that motivates this book—and indeed the work of social profit organizations—with an invitation to join me and others in creating an ever-growing collection of rubrics and commentary that will be helpful, even inspirational, to the sector.

Do you remember Humphrey Bogart walking off into the mist with Claude Rains at the end of *Casablanca*, saying, "Louis, I think this is the beginning of a beautiful friendship"? That's my hope for this book: that it will bring together people within and among social profit organizations and the many new businesses with expressed social purposes in unified efforts that will produce social profit in a troubled world.

1

A Note to the Reader

I PICTURE YOU IN VARIOUS WAYS. I imagine you working for a nonprofit or, better, a *social profit* organization in the United States or elsewhere in the world. Perhaps you lead one, or expect to lead one someday. You work for this organization because of its mission, not because you are primarily drawn to organizational life or to managing other people.

Or perhaps you work for one of the new breed of businesses with an expressed social mission—a B Corp or an L3C (low-profit, limited liability company) where the bottom line has more than one dimension. You are being asked to measure social as well as financial profit as you describe your mission and your successes.

Or I see you sitting on a social profit board. You have another job and perhaps a family, so life is full. Your training for trusteeship may not have been very extensive, but you are well aware that the governing board literally owns this organization for the benefit of the public. You are always eager for insights into how to fulfill that responsibility well.

Or maybe you are a foundation officer who invests in the efforts of staff and board members in the social sector. You are aware of the challenges they face and are always looking for ways to help the organizations you fund. You accept that there will be power dynamics between funders and grantees but wish the primary tone of the relationship were one of partnership in pursuit of social benefits.

Or perhaps you are not part of the inner workings of social profit organizations but are still part of the broadly defined civic and volunteer sectors. You are a good neighbor who wants to improve your own community, and you are willing to work informally with others toward those ends. On a philosophical level, you all care about the welfare of people you do not know, and who have not yet been born. You would like broad social and economic and political and ecological systems to function well, now and in the future. I hope you, too, are among my readers.

If you work in or govern a social profit organization, you face a variety of circumstances: from start-ups to anchor institutions; from single-person staffs to workforces of hundreds; from homogeneous groups to coalitions that cross boundaries of sectors and cultures. I envision you in Newark, San Francisco, and Grafton, Vermont, in Toronto and Rome, in New Delhi and Accra, in Sydney and Shanghai.

But for all these differences, you have much in common. You likely admire most of your colleagues on the staff and board and enjoy being with them—most of the time. You believe the work your organization does is important, and that it does it reasonably well, considering that finances are tight, and you are understaffed, and the board doesn't meet as frequently as would be ideal for an ongoing strategic conversation about the future. When it comes to your organization, you are not averse to change, but you have noticed that change is hard to bring about.

When people ask how you are, you shake your head and say, "Busy." This is no surprise, given that as a modern global citizen, you typically take in about five times as much information every day as you did just twenty-five years ago, according to information scientists—the equivalent of 175 newspapers.[5] I will urge you to draw back from that busy-ness long enough to reflect on some mind-sets and practices that will *save* you time in the end as you bring about the social profit that matters most to you.

— Who Am I? —

I am a teacher, and I have always tried to be a learner as well. I taught literature and poetry for twenty years. I was a co-founder and director (and thus chief fund-raiser) of the Mountain School of Milton Academy in Vermont, which still thrives thirty years later and has been the prototype for the creation of semester schools across the United States. I served for twelve years as president and CEO of the Geraldine R. Dodge Foundation, which established during my tenure an initiative with its grantees to provide them with ongoing professional and organizational development—usually referred to in the trade as capacity building. That initiative continues, and I am grateful to remain on its faculty.

I have lived and worked abroad, in Ghana, and I have traveled around the world twice—once on a lacrosse team representing the United States in Australia and Hong Kong, and once as a performing artist re-creating Mark Twain's global tour of the 1890s. I have been a trustee on seven governing boards, including foundations, schools, and social profit organizations. I am now a consultant to mission-based people and organizations wherever they work. From these experiences and perspectives I have an abiding interest in the humanities and great respect for the people and organizations in many cultures who strive to serve and improve the lot of humankind.

My confidence that social profit organizations can advance from *good to great* stems from the unusual combination of having spent the first half of my career in education and the second half in philanthropy. As an educator, I became familiar with rubrics as a colleague of Grant Wiggins, a leading proponent of their use in curriculum and assessment design. It was during the philanthropy years, with the help of colleagues and leaders in the social sector, that I brought the two worlds together and developed the specific content of this book. During these same years, it was the teacher in me that kept looking for what else I could learn from the privileged vantage point of a foundation president, and how I could share that learning, and indeed ways to learn, with others. This book is the result.

—— What's the Problem? ——

Imagine an executive director of a social profit organization. She is working late the night before a board meeting, completing a proposal to a local foundation, one to which she has applied before. The proposal form asks, "By what measurable outcomes will you determine the success of your work?" She repeats the metrics she reported on last year: numbers of workshops offered; number of people served; scores on evaluation forms at the end of workshops. But she can't help but feel something is missing. She would like to describe the biggest change the organization made that year, but that would mean describing the big mistake that caused it as well. Maybe not.

Imagine a new board member of that social profit organization. He is driving to the meeting the next day and glancing at the materials for the meeting, which he has just printed out. He meant to do that earlier but ran out of time. Luckily, he knows, the major points will be repeated at the meeting in the various reports, and he can pose questions if he has any. If you asked him how the organization measured its success, he might say, "Let me check the packet." If you asked him how the board measured its success as a board, or his success as a board member, he might say, "What?"

Imagine a foundation officer receiving the latest proposal from this social profit organization and re-reading the report submitted on the previous year's grant. It says the organization served twelve hundred people, a 20 percent increase from the year before. But *Is that good?* she thinks. *Should it have been 30 percent? And how well were they served?* She reads the report, which says in effect that social problems are getting worse but everything is going better than ever with this organization and the foundation should continue in its wisdom and generosity with ongoing funding. The foundation officer thinks: *This feels more like a dance than an evaluation.*

These people deserve a better assessment system. And so do the people this social profit organization serves.

Let's keep going and imagine an organization whose chief funding source is government contracts. Let's say it is a shelter for abused woman and children. The contracts are based on numbers of bed-nights per month, and that metric is the one that becomes synonymous with success. The higher the occupancy, the better job the organization is doing in the eyes of its funder. But then picture the executive director saying, "Our long-term job is not housing abused women and children; it is ensuring that no woman or child is abused." She and her colleagues help create violence prevention programs at the local high schools and the army base down the road. Fewer women and children come to the shelter for help. There are empty beds. And funding for the organization starts to diminish.

This executive director—and those women and children—need a better assessment system.

— My Argument —

I believe that how practitioners in the social sector think about measurement and assessment, and how they act upon assessment and evaluation, are the keys to increasing not only their effectiveness and impact, but also their satisfaction and pleasure in their jobs.

I want to acknowledge that when confronted with the urgent problems of the world, assessment is not the first thing that would come to mind as the key to success. For many of us, the stomach roils when the subject even comes up. Thinking about assessment feels a little like going to the dentist: We know we should do it, but it's not what we would choose to do on a sunny afternoon.

But the world around us is demanding we take a stance. We live and work in a time when there is increasing pressure to measure the results of our efforts, because money is scarce and societal needs are growing. Calls for "metrics" and "outcomes measurement" are everywhere. How should we respond? This book will make the case that it is *not* by being more "scientific" or "business-like." In my opinion, we should not focus our efforts on trying to create valid and reliable measures that "prove" the efficacy of what we have accomplished. For one thing, the social, political, and economic systems in which we operate are too complicated for us to prove anything. Even more than that, I worry that by concentrating on the measures themselves, we run the risk of taking our eyes off the real prize, which is the work itself—the *social profit* that is the reason we exist.

I will not suggest we ignore measurement—far from it. I will argue that while quantitative measures can certainly help us, qualitative measures *in addition* can help us even more. I will advocate for creating homegrown and even idiosyncratic assessment tools with your colleagues that unite everyone in your organization around a clear, shared vision of what it is you are trying to accomplish together. And I will advocate that you regard assessment not as an occasional chore but as a daily mind-set that will affect a number of behaviors, including how you spend time with one another, how you talk about your success, and how you react to setbacks.

In short, in the first half of this book, I will urge you to think of assessment not as primarily something others do to you, looking back on work you have done, but as something you do with and for yourselves as a group, focused on work that is yet to happen. Over time, I believe that this approach and these behaviors will come to shape and define your organizational culture in very positive ways.

In the second half of the book, I will profile organizations that are turning this theory into practice. I believe the road toward a more livable, more equitable, happier, healthier world begins with enhanced social profit *results*—results that are beneficial both for their own sake and in their power to influence decision making in other sectors. My argument is that those results will stem from social profit organizations first thinking differently about assessment and then *acting* accordingly through creating new assessment tools and making the time to use them.

Why would it matter? For starters, the social sector, as fragmented and undercapitalized as it is, is surprisingly large and has enormous potential for increased impact. In the United States alone, in 2007, there were over a million and a half tax-exempt organizations serving the public, employing close to 13.5 million workers (with volunteers swelling the workforce by another 4.5 million full-time-equivalent workers) and generating over $1.7 trillion in revenues.[6] (If your jaw just dropped, remember these figures include universities and hospitals, foundations and religious congregations.) The vast majority of social profit organizations are small, but they have an enormous impact on the lives of those they serve.

The real reason it matters is that the world desperately needs the social benefits these organizations individually and collectively produce. In our first conversation in the elevator, I said the world's a mess. I don't want to be glib about that or particularly political. I am talking about the challenges of the twenty-first century that *The New York Times* and *The Wall Street Journal* agree about: military conflicts; religious extremism; spread of diseases; persistent racism; growing income and education gaps; lack of faith in governments; extreme and destructive weather events. There is for many a sense of unraveling, a feeling that the ways we are organized to deal with problems, react to challenges, and make decisions are not sufficient to meet these challenges.[7] And partly as a result, there is also a growing, global effort that asserts that part of the problem is that we are measuring the wrong things.[8] I agree.

When I said in the elevator that I thought the civic sector could lead us out of this mess we are in, I was not suggesting that the sector has the power, wealth, and influence of the corporate and government sectors. It does not. But I am saying that by expanding their approach to measuring success, social profit organizations have the best shot at defining a better world for us all, because social profit is their reason for being.

The public and corporate sectors are full of good people who care about others. Yet in the end, social aspirations notwithstanding, those in business, particularly big business accountable to shareholders, must focus on financial profit, and those in politics must focus on power, or on staying elected, or on simply functioning in a system compromised by conflict and bureaucracy. It is those organizations whose missions are about *social* profit that have the chance—and the responsibility—to bring other purposes and values to the forefront.

— From *I* to *We* —

A story will help me illustrate what I mean. In May 2002, a coalition of foundations and civic, environmental, and business groups from New York and New Jersey sponsored a gathering called The Waterfront Conference, with part of the proceedings taking place in the train terminal in Hoboken, New Jersey, and the rest at the World Financial Center in Lower Manhattan. The purpose was to "address the inter-related needs of the region's waterfront." As the leader of one of New Jersey's major environmental foundations, I was asked to introduce Governor Jim McGreevey to a crowd of several hundred people in the vast, echoing Hoboken Terminal.

I decided to introduce the governor with a poem. Whether that was a brave or foolhardy act matters less to me than the images of the poem, which I can't quite get out of my head. As I began, the noise of ongoing conversations and metal chairs being adjusted on bare floors was substantial. But after simply saying I wanted to introduce the governor not with biographical details but with an *idea*, I started reading Adrienne Rich's poem *In Those Years*:[9]

> *In those years, people will say, we lost track*
> *of the meaning of we, of you*
> *we found ourselves*
> *reduced to I*
> *and the whole thing became*
> *silly, ironic, terrible:*
> *we were trying to live a personal life*
> *and, yes, that was the only life*
> *we could bear witness to*

The line "silly, ironic, terrible" quieted people down a bit, since the words were not expected in an introduction of a governor. It was the second stanza, though, that I thought would really capture them. I glanced at the governor, hoping he was ready to be blown away by the upcoming metaphor. For this was 2002 in New York and New Jersey, and the events of 9/11 were still fresh and the emotions raw. The governor was simultaneously looking at his notes and listening to an aide whispering in his ear as I resumed:

> *But the great dark birds of history screamed and plunged*
> *into our personal weather*
> *They were headed somewhere else but their beaks and*
> *   pinions drove*
> *along the shore, through the rags of fog*
> *where we stood, saying I*

Adrienne Rich wrote *In Those Years* in 1991, a decade before the dark birds plunged into the World Trade Center towers. But the poem seemed prescient to me, and its theme of the need to move from *I* to *We* seemed perfect for the occasion, indeed for the post-9/11 times. I felt as if I were handing the metaphor to the governor. I see in my notes that in full obsequious mode, I even referred to him as a man "uniquely suited to lead us from *I* to *We*."

He took the podium and said, "Wow. Poetry," in a tone he might have used if he had been introduced in another unexpected language: *Wow. Mandarin.* Not surprisingly, there was no mention in his following remarks of the theme of the poem. I don't blame him; he had been studying his notes right up to the last second, and he operated in a political world, not a poetic one. I had no basis for saying that he was about to lead us from *I* to *We*, except my wish it might be so—and he wasn't listening anyway.

I chastised myself for the naïveté of treating a public gathering about the future of one of the world's most important waterfronts, with a lot of money at stake, as if it were an English class. But a few hours later, an acquaintance caught my arm as we were filing out of the terminal. "That poem was the best part of the morning," he said. He was the executive director of an environmental social profit organization.

His response to the poem did not surprise me, because the questions of the poem are the ones his job asks him to think about all the time. Finding the right balance or range on the spectrum from *I* to *We* strikes me as being at the heart of an ongoing, essentially humanist quest for a better world. How can we personally thrive in a world where others are also thriving? How can we enjoy the beauties and bounties of the earth without wrecking it for our children, grandchildren, and people yet to be born? These are the kind of questions the social sector ponders.

My argument is that learning how to create better qualitative assessment tools can turn that pondering into effective action. I believe that using those tools will help social profit organizations better fulfill their missions and widen their spheres of influence, not only on the other sectors but also on consumers and voters who can underscore and deepen that influence. We can't, however, jump directly into creating new assessment tools. It won't work. To proceed requires us first to examine assumptions in a number of key areas: about what can and can't be measured; about why assessment matters; and about what uses of time are most advantageous to us individually and collectively. That is the purpose of the next three chapters.

2

Can Social Profit Be Measured?

How WE THINK ABOUT ASSESSMENT is significantly affected by how we think about measurement. We have already noted that social profit does not have a standard unit of measure, like a dollar, a centimeter, or an ounce, and thus is difficult to measure. Some would say it is impossible to measure. Yet talk of measurement is everywhere in the social sector. The public and politicians question the efficacy of the sector and ask for proof of results. Board members seek ways to assess progress over time. Funders ask for hard evidence of impact. Conferences offer panels on the subject of measurement, and a burgeoning literature offers advice. Much of the talk has to do with "metrics" and "outcomes," and technology has given us the chance to gather, analyze, and present data as never before.

As a result, most organizations in the social sector choose key metrics and keep track of them. We describe our goals in numbers, and indeed, metrics can be important. The case for further investment in social rather than financial profit is bolstered by a body of metrics associated with key indicators: percentage of a population suffering from diabetes or obesity; percentage of young men in prison in the United States, of which races and ethnicities; parts per million of carbon in the atmosphere; number and size of farms being managed sustainably; a nation's score on the UN's index of "material well-being of children"; data on infant mortality and life expectancy. The list goes on.

Yes, metrics can focus our attention and increase our motivation. But as we know, setting targets does not necessarily help us meet them. We must ask whether this data is making our organizations any better in our internal workings and in fulfilling our missions. Put another way: In an age of complex, interlocking social challenges, how should we respond to the call for more and better measurement—indeed, the expectation of it? I think we need to answer that question, not because we are primarily interested in measurement but because we are vitally interested in the success of our individual and collective efforts.

—— Who Measures What and Why? ——

When I was at the Dodge Foundation, I remember interviewing the founder and executive director of an organization in Newark that offered an arts education program designed to be a deep, transformational experience. Anecdotal evidence suggested that it was; the program seemed to be profoundly changing the lives of the young people who participated. Yet the ED was holding his head in his hands as he told me about a recent visit from another foundation officer, a key backer of this program: "All he said to me was, 'You have to get your numbers up. You have to get your numbers up.'"

Does the number of kids in a program trump the quality of the program when assessing whether or not it is successful? It can and often does if there is no *qualitative* assessment that defines a different vision of success. For better or worse, measurement becomes a proxy for intention and values.[10] It is hard to argue with the foundation officer's intention to serve as many young people as possible. But that was not the executive director's intention, certainly not his highest aspiration. He did not have the capacity to do that. He did have the capacity, and it was his mission, to change some number of young lives through the arts. But there was no metric for what mattered most to him, nothing with which to make an alternative case.

This is a familiar story. In workshops with social profit leaders, I sometimes ask, "Do you feel you are measuring what matters?" and more often than not, I get a quick no. Frequently, they say they did not think they had the option to measure what matters to them—and besides, they say, it wouldn't be a valid measure, would it? This is a critical question. At least part of the moral of the story is that if you do not define and assess what matters to you, someone else will do the assessing of your work, based on what is important to them. The other part involves an assumption and a question: What holds us back from thinking our internal, homegrown assessment would have legitimacy? Why are we so afraid of the word *soft* when applied to a measurement? It's an adjective you want to avoid if you are a politician talking about crime or a marine doing anything, but I don't think it is necessarily a bad quality for a measurement. Much that we care about—feelings of belonging, pride in citizenship, confidence in the future, a general sense of well-being—requires soft measurements. The real question is whether those measures can help us *achieve* what we care about.

— Validity and Reliability —

We live in an age when measurement and its uses in assessment and evaluation have become a serious science. Indeed, when a measure itself has to meet standards—think of the SAT or the Richter scale—we quite properly train our attention on those standards. Is it accurate? Is it reliable, which is to say does it give consistent results? Is it valid, which is to say does it measure what it is supposed to measure? These criteria are extremely important if a carpenter is measuring for a shelf, or a coach is weighing in wrestlers before a tournament, or a doctor is drawing blood to determine levels of uric acid.

But does a measure always have to meet strict criteria to be helpful? I think we get confused over whether it is the measure that matters or what is being measured. We get intimidated by the science of measurement, forgetting that, in the words of change expert Michael Fullan, "Statistics are a wonderful servant and an appalling master."[11] We find ourselves arguing over whether a measure of levels of quality can ever be accurate or valid. But what if we were able to agree that a measure is accurate *enough*, or valid and reliable *enough*, for us to take sensible and appropriate action based on what we learn from it?

This question is important because we know any measure of social profit will never have the consistency we seek in standardized measures, nor the precision. I know from the foundation perspective how difficult it is to compare the outcomes of two different arts education programs, let alone weigh the relative benefits of preserving a hundred acres of farmland or providing "talking circles" for troubled adolescents. But I also know how enthusiastically we responded to our grantees who had a process for identifying community needs, priorities, values, and visions, and who described in detail their aspirations and their plans for achieving them. We did not talk about criteria of validity and reliability, because they were not the main point. We were basing our social investments on something else—a clear *process* that led to clear benefits, even if those benefits were described in words instead of defined by numbers.

— Measurement and Accountability —

I remember a time early in my career, when my wife and I founded the semester program at the Mountain School, and we were scheduled to have our first visit from the State of Vermont. I prepared voluminous material about the new educational program and was excited to talk about its innovations: the way the English and science courses were taught in relation to each other and to our rural environment; the use of student journals for personal reflection and group process; the three-day solo camping trip; the work program; the student-led morning meetings.

You must be shaking your head at my innocence. The visit focused on two things: whether the furnaces were safe, and whether the kitchen was up to code.

This was my introduction to the idea that while program performance may be foremost in the minds of social profit leaders, it may not be in the minds of their outside assessors. Indeed, social profit organizations are accountable in at least two major areas aside from program performance: keeping their operations legal; and appropriately managing their finances.[12] And because many social profit organizations receive government funding, they soon learn what governments value most—compliance with minimum standards in these areas, defined by law.

The danger of this situation is obvious. In a sector where many organizations and leaders are struggling to survive, they respond first to the immediate incentives in front of them to be compliant in all legal matters and in financial accounting and reporting. This compliance takes more time than we have, and we get used to the idea that assessment and evaluation come from the outside world. But the outside world, particularly government, is not pushing on quality of work or level of service to clients and constituents, because they don't have a measure for it beyond numbers served. There is no law that we have to be great at what we do.

We should train ourselves to ask, *Whom does this measurement serve?* I'll never forget the first time I realized as a teacher that the primary purpose of the SAT was not to help my students; it was to help adults choose among them. Similarly, traditional outside measures of the work of individual social profit organizations are not designed for them; they are designed to make distinctions among them. So, surprisingly, measuring program performance seriously, honestly, rigorously, continuously, in a way that can inform and improve our work, is up to us. It is critically important to do so despite the dearth of outside incentives, because that is where social profit lies. Chapters 5 and 6 of this book will describe at least one way to do it.

— Measuring What Matters —

It is helpful when thinking about measurement to remember the lines often attributed to Albert Einstein: "Everything that can be counted does not necessarily count; everything that counts cannot necessarily be counted."[13]

I am arguing that there are particular kinds of social profit that resist quantification, that resist standard measures, that are hard to pin down because they are dynamic in themselves, but are at the heart of how we imagine our missions being realized in the world. Faced with the realization that we will *never* find a common unit for these visions of social profit, we have two choices. We can say it cannot be measured, or we can measure it ourselves in the manner that social profit demands: a combination of pertinent metrics and a qualitative description of that social profit *that can only be created by the people who are providing and receiving it*. We must envision and define and then reflect and redefine these visions of success, believing that "if you measure what you value, people will value what you measure." I believe we can do it if we start thinking differently about assessment, which is the topic of the next chapter.

3

Thinking Differently About Assessment

THE PHRASE THINKING DIFFERENTLY invites the question, *From what?* I believe that most of us have a deep, usually unexamined assumption that assessment is something others do *to us* after we have performed in some way, as opposed to something we do *for ourselves*, for our own future ends. I believe we can and must adopt a different stance. Since how we *think* about assessment now and in the future plays such a big part in my argument, let's draw back and ask how we think about anything.

— What's in Our Heads? —

Cognitive science reminds us that whenever we turn to a new topic, it matters what is already in our heads—the existing knowledge, assumptions, and conceptual frameworks, the mental models through which we understand the world.

What happens when the world demands our attention and a response?[14] The stimulus comes in from our environment, and our consciousness, our working memory, tries to deal with it. The working memory is finite and can get overwhelmed. Fortunately, it has remarkable access to something much bigger, our long-term memory, which you can imagine as a huge file drawer—or if you are younger, a hard drive—that contains facts, knowledge, processes, experiences, assumptions, biases, you name it.

So if I ask, "What color is blood?" your working memory checks with the long-term memory and says, "Red." You weren't thinking about *red* but suddenly there it was. If I ask, "What is four times three?" you say "Twelve." It wasn't a number sitting there waiting for you to retrieve it, it was a process: multiplication.

But what if I said, "Tell me what this statement means: *The notes were sour because the seams were split.*" When I flash those words on a screen at a workshop, all around me I see people eyeing the exits and signaling, *Don't call on me.* But then I add a picture of a man playing the bagpipes, followed by the words again, *The notes were sour because the seams were split.* Suddenly the sentence makes sense, and everyone exhales (whatever lingering questions remain about the functioning of bagpipes).

What just happened? It's a quick illustration of something we intuitively know and cognitive scientists explain: The way we see and understand the world is affected by what is already in our heads. We are not blank slates. For most things we already have a frame of reference.

So we must ask: What is in our heads regarding *assessment?* I ask you: *What are your associations with the word* assessment? *What has been your experience with the word, and how do you feel about assessment?* I urge you to pause and ponder your answers and ask yourself what assumptions you have as a result—assumptions that are lurking in your long-term memory to affect your thinking and behavior.

When I ask these questions in workshops, people tend to agree that our experience with and assumptions about assessment are not very helpful to us, particularly as we grapple with questions of assessment and evaluation in our current jobs. At their most benign, our assumptions limit the ways we can imagine using assessment to improve our work. At their worst, they give us a visceral negative reaction to the word. Why? I think it is because we all went to school.

Imagine your high school teachers lined up before you, and ask them to give you a synonym for *assessment*. What would they say? Most people respond quickly: "Test." In fact, our longest-standing experience with assessment comes from tests, quizzes, and exams. Lots of them. And all those experiences placed an assumption deep in our bones: Assessment comes at the end, and it judges how we did.

We should not underestimate how our experience in school has affected our assumptions about the purpose of assessment. As we experienced it, again and again, assessment in its various forms seemed to exist for the purpose of judging (and recording) how we did. It was not about learning, because it came after the supposed learning had taken place. In its most extreme form of standardized testing, it was clearly distinct from our actual schoolwork; it seemed to be more about sorting kids into winners and losers.

We should also not underestimate the effects of experiencing assessment as a series of judgments. A pattern of judgments can limit our sense of what we can or should do next. It can close down opportunities rather than open them up. This kind of assessment *can* serve as a motivator, for sure, and it is certainly possible to be motivated by both learning and doing well on a test. But how often do we hear students say, "I learned a lot from that" after a test?

Let's propose a different assumption: *The primary purpose of assessment is to improve performance.*[15] That changes everything. And with it comes the idea that we can take assessment into our own hands, not just as individuals but as groups committed to common goals.

When I used to conduct assessment workshops at schools, there were two groups of adults who intuitively understood this assumption about the primary purpose of assessment and used it as a principle in their interaction with students: coaches and teachers of performing arts. This makes perfect sense, for their work is all about student performance, not the subject being covered. Imagine a coach saying to a basketball player after losing a championship game by one point, "I'm not surprised you missed those last two foul shots, because you have had your feet too close together since the first day of practice." Or a drama teacher saying to a lead actor at the cast party after the final performance, "You know why the audience didn't react to the climatic line of the play? They couldn't hear you. You've been turning your back to them for the last two weeks." Unthinkable.

Instead, the assessment of students in sports and performing arts is frequent, individualized, and ungraded. It is not about judgment; it is aimed at ambitious, well-understood performances that are coming up soon—the games, the recitals, and the plays. It makes explicit the gaps between current performance and the level of performance you are aiming for. The assessment efforts are aimed at the future, not the past, and the people being assessed know where they are heading.

If we are lucky, we can remember other teachers who acted more like coaches—who concentrated on what we could *do* with our knowledge and skills in history or biology, rather than on how much of the textbook we could recall. They let us perform, gave us feedback on how we were doing along the way, then let us try again. But the vast majority of us, as students and adults, have experienced assessment as an audit of past performance rather than as helpful coaching in preparation for our next endeavors.

I am not suggesting assessment should *never* audit or judge performance. Auditing is helpful in communicating and enforcing minimum standards—whether a student has done the reading, or a building has a safe furnace, or an organization has its financial house in order. Organizations need *summative* assessment systems—systems that are about rating and judging—if, for instance, there is some doubt whether someone should keep his job. And when there is a scarce resource such as admission to a highly selective college, a standardized assessment spreads students out on a scale. We will never get away from these uses of assessment.

Yet because assessment is legitimately used to ensure minimum standards or make decisions about hiring and firing or determine who wins admission to Stanford does not mean it can only be used that way. At the heart of thinking differently about assessment is the belief that it can do a different job as well, which is to help us gain clarity about what we aspire to accomplish together and bolster our efforts to perform at the highest levels in the areas that matter most to us. Then assessment does not come at the end. It precedes action. It is at the heart of planning for the future. It is formative, not summative. And it is in our hands, not those of others.

— Planning Backward —

The Geraldine R. Dodge Foundation offers its grantees a six-month-long board leadership series, which begins with a session on assessment. This year, for the first time in over twelve years of leading that workshop, I decided not to mention the word *assessment* until we were well into the topic.

Instead, I asked three questions, with a few minutes in between them so people could write down their answers. Try it:

1. Given your organization, with its particular mission, what would success look like for you in the next three to five years? Use metrics if they are helpful, but feel free to *describe* what you would like to see. (pause)
2. Whatever you just wrote, can you be more specific? (pause)
3. If you haven't already done so, would you give an example of what you've just written about?

Then I asked people to compare notes with others from their same organization.

The energy level in the room was high at this point—and why wouldn't it be? Everyone was talking with a colleague, sometimes two or three, about why the organization they work for, or volunteer for, exists in the world. People wanted to keep talking, but I stopped them and asked them to write down their responses to three more questions, again with a few minutes to ponder each:

4. Whatever success looked like for you in that last set of questions, now describe what it would look like at an even higher level. Put another way, what would success *really* look like in the next three to five years? (pause)
5. Whatever you just wrote, can you be more specific? (pause)
6. If you don't have an example to help me and others understand what you mean by success at this level, would you make one up?

Again, I asked each organizational team to compare notes. And let's just say the energy level was *really* high. I could have left the room for half an hour at this point without anyone noticing. But instead, after a while, I asked, "Is this a good conversation?" *Yes*, the group answered. "Would you like to bring your other staff and board colleagues in on it?" *Yes*.

There is a tool that helps people organize and elaborate upon the answers to these questions—the rubric—and we were at an early stage of rubric writing here (the topic of chapter 5), without mentioning the word. People were describing the social profit at the heart of their missions or the level of high functioning that would bring it about, and it was time to introduce the concept of *planning backward*. How is that different from planning ahead? Planning ahead is making a dinner reservation; planning backward is picturing yourself making a toast at the dinner and remembering the guest of honor has a favorite poet and memorizing a poem for the occasion. Put another way, you can plan ahead to be at the dinner, but you need to plan backward (or ought to) if you are going to *perform* at the dinner. Planning ahead is deciding to go to Spain for vacation; planning backward is picturing yourself interacting with servers in an out-of-the-way restaurant and then purchasing some tapes or enrolling in a basic language class. Your vision of success had you conversing in a language you didn't know, so you were then able to plan backward to learn some of it before you landed in your vacation spot.

Planning backward is the *sine qua non* of formative assessment. Again, it is not a new or strange idea, but I believe we do not plan backward often enough, in a sustained and systematic way, with our staff and board colleagues. To do so, we have to have identified what matters most to us as a group collectively dedicated to a particular social mission. Planning backward forces us to focus on our primary values and our highest aspirations for the impact of our work—the specific social profit we are designed to create. And it changes what we do. It changes how we perform.

Let me give some examples of planning backward in action, beginning with a personal one: the evolution of the book you hold in your hands. When I began this project, I had a reasonable but modest answer to the question of what success would look like. I wanted to create a workbook to sustain the momentum of the Dodge Foundation workshops. I wanted to help with follow-up, because I knew how difficult it is for people who have attended any workshop to bring ideas home. If they come home fired up to change anything in their workplace, their colleagues usually avoid them until the enthusiasm wanes and they give up. Even if they find colleagues receptive to new ideas, it is hard for people new to ideas themselves to teach them to others. So I wanted to help my friends in New Jersey, where our foundation focused its work.

But I followed my own advice and asked what success would *really* look like. I thought, *Why not try to be helpful to social profit organizations in other parts of the United States and elsewhere?*

That led me to apply for and receive a writer's residency at The Rockefeller Foundation's Bellagio Center on Lake Como in Italy, which afforded me not only some protected time to write but also the opportunity to confer with artists and scholars and social profit leaders from around the world, which continued to expand my ambitions. I stopped picturing a workbook and began picturing a full-bodied resource—a book.

Planning backward is a good and potentially powerful idea for any project, and in my case it did not need an assessment tool to influence or direct my decisions. However, for more complex performances with multiple players, the assessment tool is crucial. Let's look, for example, at LEED (Leadership in Energy and Environmental Design), a rating system overseen by the US Green Building Council. Since its beginnings in 1998, LEED has evolved into a set of ratings that address all aspects of green buildings, from design and construction to operations and maintenance, and in contexts ranging from renovations to new construction to the scale of neighborhoods.

How does planning backward work with LEED? Let's imagine a question—I would consider it an assessment question—that might be broached in almost any meeting of staff and board at a social profit organization: *Does our space reflect our values?* Organizations with environmental missions will see the immediate relevance of that question to them, and the circle widens when people become aware that designers of green buildings emphasize human health as much as energy efficiency.

So *Yes, we ought to have a green building*, some number of those organizations decide. Then what? The next step is not to call a contractor and start building. It is to ask some assessment questions: *What qualifies a building as green? What are the criteria by which reasonable people would judge the success of this upcoming project? How can we learn from other organizations that have gone green? In our case, with our specific mission and needs and hierarchy of values, what should we be planning backward from?*

Happily, LEED provides an extensive answer in the form of an assessment tool that awards points for component parts of green. This information is provided in advance, and the criteria for success are transparent. If an organization seeks LEED certification, it plans backward from the LEED scale and makes certain decisions it might not otherwise have made, because its idea of what success means has become more detailed and specific.

The LEED scale in use when I was working on creating a green building for the Dodge Foundation had lots of criteria for scoring LEED points, including the following credits, each worth a point toward achieving a certified, silver, gold, or platinum level of accomplishment:

> *Credit 5.1 Local/Regional Materials, 20% manufactured locally*
> *Credit 5.2 Local/Regional Materials, of 20% above, 50% harvested locally*

It might not be immediately obvious why this matters. If you are building in New Jersey, what difference does it make if your hardwood floors come from eastern Pennsylvania or British Columbia? What if there's a great sale on the wood from Canada; shouldn't you look for the best deal? The LEED scale offers an answer: You get points if you avoid the extra energy expended in lengthy transportation. The goal is not just to rack up points to achieve a higher LEED rating; it's to keep focused on your initial aim. In the absence of the clear value placed on energy efficiency in all phases of the building project, we would default to our usual criterion for success: low cost.

The person who ordered the local/regional materials was not suddenly smarter, or better, or more moral than anyone else—she was operating within an assessment system that told her what to do. We will see numerous other examples of how planning backward affects our decisions in chapters 7 through 9 of this book.

Suffice it to say that if you decide what matters to you and take the time to describe what performance looks like in relation to what you value, you can start to measure how close you come to your vision of success. Unlike many other performances, you do not have to become more *skilled* to succeed; you need to have clarified *collectively* what it is you are trying to accomplish. And if hurdles like cost barriers get in the way, this process will provide you with the tools to evaluate and act upon your priorities.

The LEED answer to the question of what success looks like in green building comes from the outside. You may or may not agree with its conclusions, and you can reserve the right to place different weight on different criteria than the LEED scale does—after all, it's your building. The LEED rating scales evolve as more is learned about green building practices and as there are advances in technologies and materials. That's a good thing. Rating scales should evolve; when our answer to what success looks like, and our achievements, become ever more ambitious, it indicates that our assessment tools, too, have been a success.

More often than not, you do not have an external measure as definitive or widely accepted as the LEED scale. Planning backward begins with your own vision, which can be developed in sufficient detail if you have allotted time for the task (see chapter 4).

Let's look at an organization that took that time. Trust for Public Land (TPL), a US-based environmental organization, asked me to make a presentation on formative assessment practices to a national leadership group at a retreat center in Wisconsin. TPL's staff protects lands and creates parks across the nation, so they navigate many land deals in the name of conservation. They had already been discussing what they most valued in a conservation deal, and they were frustrated that the only criteria of success for any given deal were the ones easiest to measure: number of acres conserved, and number of dollars leveraged from other sources. These were important measures to be sure, but not all that mattered to them. When they asked themselves what a conservation deal that most

fully expressed their values looked like, they came up with criteria
for success that went far beyond the deal itself:

• Previously underserved location and/or people
• Civic engagement in the process
• Current and anticipated learning opportunities
• Anticipated use by people
• Effect on community economics
• Effects on environmental health

The values of TPL are very clear in this list. But just stating the
values did not allow them to measure what matters in relation to
them. Might it be possible to assign a range of possible points in
each area, similar to the LEED scale, not in order to win an award
or level of certification but rather to strive for maximum value as
defined by the group itself?

In fact, that is what happened. In the months following our
workshop, the folks at TPL created a remarkable assessment tool,
with the input of hundreds of staff members working in offices
across the country. In chapter 9, I will tell the story of how that
assessment tool evolved and has been revised and adopted since by
other organizations and for other purposes.

With a clear, specific, shared vision to plan backward from,
an organization can engage with another concept that is critical
to formative assessment—feedback. The more specific the shared
vision of success is, the more likely it is you can give and receive
feedback along the way toward reaching that vision. But first we
have to rehabilitate the word.

— Getting Feedback —

When I want to make the point that, like *assessment*, this suppos-
edly benign word *feedback* needs rehabilitating, I create a quick

scenario with a participant in my workshop, pretending we work together and haven't seen each other for a few days. We approach each other as if coming down a hallway from different directions. "Tony," I say, "I'm glad I bumped into you. I've been meaning to give you a little feedback."

Inevitably, nervous laughter ripples through the room. When I ask why, Tony says, "I must have done something wrong," and others say, "This is not good," or "You look friendly, but you're about to criticize him."

This emotional reaction is not inherent in the word *feedback*; it is the result of our using the word as code for giving advice or criticism, well intended or not. We are not operating in a feedback *system*—which is to say the feedback is not part of a larger, organized, overall approach. And we can't create a system unless we've decided what's important, where we are headed, and what we want to see along the way. We can't give or receive real feedback unless we *both* know what we are planning backward from.

You can check you own assumptions about feedback by simply finishing this sentence Grant Wiggins used to pose to teachers: "To be exemplary feedback, it must be _____."
When I ask a roomful of people from the social sector to fill in that blank, the answers fall into two categories. The first contains words like *honest*, *tactful*, and *useful*. There's nothing wrong with these words, but I expect they come to mind because of what feedback has not been for these people rather than from an understanding of what it might be at its best. Why wouldn't feedback be honest, for example? Or why might a blunt appraisal, however accurate, come across as tactless? Because the people involved haven't agreed upon the purpose of the feedback. They don't have a mutual focus on improving a performance that matters.

It is possible for honest, tactful, and specific feedback on performance to still not be useful. Take an English teacher bending over backward to be gentle with a student during a paper conference: "Sally, you are showing real improvement here. The paper has a much clearer thesis statement than your last one did, and you use some great detail from the story in your second paragraph. I think you need to refer to the text in the rest of the body paragraphs, too, though. And you lose me a little bit here at the end, in the sentence that begins with *However*. It almost seems like you are contradicting what you said on the first page. I think you were more careful in general this time, but there are still too many spelling errors. Even one is too many. Okay?"

She leaves thinking, *I knew Mr. Grant didn't like me.* The teacher is thinking feedback. The student is hearing judgment. He is trying to be helpful. She is waiting for praise or blame. They hadn't taken the time to set up a system in which the feedback could work.

The second group of responses to the unfinished sentence implies what Wiggins calls an actual feedback *system*, one that is more likely to help because it is *descriptive, contextual*, and *timely*. With this second set of adjectives, we don't have to say feedback should be "useful." It is useful by design. It is descriptive as opposed to judgmental, contextual because we have created the context, and timely because we design our feedback system to give and receive it in time to use it.

Getting good at formative assessment requires a shared definition of feedback. Here is mine: *Feedback is specific information, in the form of descriptive comments or data, that illuminates the effectiveness of current levels of performance in relation to desired levels. The levels are defined by the person or organization receiving the feedback. The information arrives in time to help improve or adjust performance, as needed.*

With this definition, Tony wouldn't be trying to escape me in that hallway; he would welcome the information. He might have even been looking for me in order to get it. .

As you consider this definition yourselves, you might decide that you don't get as much "real" feedback as you would like. Social profit organizations hear from a small group of stalwart friends and frequent critics all the time—and it is tempting to consider those voices as sufficient feedback. But if we want the potential benefits of hearing from people we do not run across every day, or getting data that does not come to us easily, then we have to design the system that gives us the information we want in time to use it. And that in itself takes time.

Let me state the obvious: You can't design anything, especially together with your colleagues, if you haven't designated the time to do the work. In fact, I don't think it is possible to move from theory to practice in formative assessment without acknowledging this reality and acting accordingly, which is the topic of chapter 4.

4

Mission Time

WHERE DO WE BEGIN WITH FORMATIVE ASSESSMENT? I used to think the proper starting point was developing clarity about mission, goals, and criteria for success. But experience working closely with scores of organizations has convinced me otherwise. Now I think we need to begin with *time*. Just as we stepped back and considered the word *assessment*, we need to ask how we consciously and unconsciously think about time.

There's a line in Aldous Huxley's novel *Brave New World* that I love. It occurs at the end of a chapter, when the character known as the Savage has undergone a ritual manhood initiation, a kind of mock crucifixion, and he collapses to the ground. Huxley writes, "He had discovered Time and Death and God." Yes! That is exactly where time belongs, on a list with death and God—things that are beyond human control, and perhaps human comprehension. Yet time is the most important resource we have in our work; it is the essential currency of our lives.

A generation ago, in his book *The 7 Habits of Highly Effective People*, Stephen Covey presented a helpful way of thinking about time—the Urgent/Important matrix. He created four quadrants, as shown in table 4.1, and asked readers where they generally spend their time.

Table 4.1: The Covey Matrix

	URGENT	NOT URGENT
IMPORTANT	Quadrant I: Everything is Important and Urgent	Quadrant II: Everything is Important but not Urgent
NOT IMPORTANT	Quadrant III: Nothing is Important but matters are still Urgent	Quadrant IV: Matters are neither Important nor Urgent

The vast majority of people who work in the social profit sector say their work lives are based in Quadrant I. Most of their efforts, driven by mission, meaning, and values, feel important. But they also feel urgent, if not late and overdue. The social needs their organizations address are pressing, even overwhelming, and there sometimes seems to be barely enough time to breathe. Quadrant I is the burn-out quadrant.

People in my workshops say that when they are not in Quadrant I, they are in Quadrant III, dealing with tasks that don't feel important to them but are urgent for someone else. This is a demoralizing quadrant. Occasionally, they admit, they retreat to Quadrant IV, which often involves some combination of a sofa, alcohol, and cable television. You get fired if you spend too much time in this quadrant.

That leaves Quadrant II. Covey asks if we could just do one or two things more consistently in our personal lives, what would they be? Whenever I have asked that question, people say the same things: exercise; reading for pleasure; spending time with a spouse or partner; keeping in touch with old friends; having a hobby. They are all Quadrant II activities.

Are they important? Yes. Are they urgent? No. That's why we don't get to them. When asked why we don't do these things more often, we answer, "Because I don't have enough time." But Covey's matrix helps us understand that it is really because they are not urgent. They can be put off without immediate consequences. We spend our time in Quadrants I and III because the work is, often literally, right in our faces. Yet longer-term, our lives are diminished by not spending enough time in Quadrant II.

How do people we know actually accomplish important, non-urgent activities on a regular basis? They schedule time for them, and that time is inviolate. This is a crucial insight for my purposes, for while Covey is trying to get us to think about Quadrant II *as individuals*, I want us to think about it as organizations. *We cannot shift our thinking and practice surrounding assessment without recognizing that formative assessment is a Quadrant II activity.*

Ironically then, the first step in formative assessment has nothing to do with assessment. It is about understanding the need to designate time for the work. Again, I used to wait until the end of my workshops to raise the issue of how organizations use time. Now I begin with it. The work of creating a formative assessment tool, let alone a formative assessment system, let alone a formative assessment culture, simply will not happen unless organizations schedule time for it and protect that time from the other more urgent demands upon it. I suggest finding a name for this important-but-not-urgent time that is all your own. Maybe you could name it after a founder or a landmark or a key word in your mission. From now on, I will refer to it as *mission time* and leave it to you to personalize it from there.

I fervently believe that mission time calms you down and saves you other time in the long run. Mission time is where we can achieve thoughtful clarity about who we are, what we are going to do and not going to do, what we do best, and how we will go about it. We can ask how the world is changing around us and reflect on how we will know whether we are being successful in it.

The way the social sector works, mission time is usually scarce. Organizations are funded for projects, not operations. Strategic decisions are made by executive directors late at night instead of by working groups with time to talk through options and imagine alternative approaches. Lack of mission time, in my opinion, is why so many thoughtful and even inspiring strategic plans do not bring about the changes they describe. The plans were created in retreat mode, but there is not ongoing time of the same quality devoted to their implementation.

I now tell people at my workshops that if the leaders of their organizations don't support identifying, protecting, and learning to use mission time, they should not bother to approach their assessment practices any differently. It would be too discouraging, even painful. Put more positively, leaders must insist on mission time, and they must be patient and help others be patient as the organization learns how to use it well. They will know they are leading an assessment culture when no one in the organization can imagine doing without it.

— Using Mission Time —

Once organizations embrace the goals of formative assessment and set aside mission time, they are on the road to more organized and targeted learning and more focused, flexible, and effective performance. I make the case in chapter 5 that one of the highest and best uses of mission time is creating new assessment tools in the form of qualitative assessment rubrics. But there are other excellent ways to spend this time together. Here are some ideas.

Gathering and interpreting information.

One of the benefits of mission time is that it allows people who work together to ask, *Is there any information we don't have that we should have?* Inevitably, the answer is yes, and then they can figure out how to get it. Surveys and questionnaires, for example, can provide excellent information on current realities, preferences, and opinions of a selected population of people. Focus groups, where you sit down with a representative group of people affected by your work, can give you very direct and helpful feedback, along with new ideas and relationships. There are numerous sources on how to design these tools; I will just note here that the more you habitually seek and *use* feedback, the higher the response rate will be to surveys, and the better the food, the better the focus group. With new information at your disposal, you can use mission time to ask, *What does this tell us, and what should we do about it?*

Diagnosing the current situation.

The sturdiest exercise for determining what's going on with your organization and what needs attention is the SWOT (Strengths/Weaknesses/Opportunities/Threats) analysis. Simply ask, *At this moment in our organization's history, what are our Strengths, and what are our Weaknesses? What Opportunities do we see in the near future, and what are the potential Threats to our achieving our mission?* Have people answer these questions individually, then discuss their answers in small groups, then report out to the whole group. Patterns will emerge, and questions: *How do we maintain our strengths? How do we address our weaknesses? How do we seize the most important opportunities within our reach? How do we minimize the threats to our work?*

Having some purposeful fun.

One of my favorite uses of mission time, particularly in a retreat setting, is a planning backward exercise. This particular exercise is best done in small groups, deliberately mixing up people from different departments or, in the case of larger organizations, locations. At organizational retreats, you can have board/staff teams. Tell each group: *Imagine that five years from now, our organization is on the cover of a magazine. Choose the magazine, design the cover and headline, and write the first paragraph or two of the article.* When you compare the results, you may start to hear, "We can do that," and you will be planning backward from an ambitious vision.

All of the activities above provide information and momentum for what I believe is the single most effective use of mission time: *designing your own assessment rubrics*. Rubrics, as you will see, define levels of performance along a spectrum, in relation to the most important criteria for success, as determined by those who know the work most intimately. Rubrics can certainly contain metrics where numbers are helpful, but they also contain words—as many of them as you need to clarify what you are trying to do and help you achieve the results you are after. They become the physical representation of a long-term commitment to formative assessment, and they provide a context for ongoing individual and organizational self-evaluation.

Organizations that embrace formative assessment also embrace the idea of local assessment design. They recognize that while some performances are defined and enhanced by standardized measures, such as number of meals served or acres preserved, there are other performances that are specific to their own mission and geography and clientele. They see the potential power and impact of customizing instruments that describe and measure the levels of performances and accomplishments to which *they* aspire, based on their own mission, values, and goals.

Here's a quick recap: Chapter 2 asks you to consider whether something that cannot be precisely quantified could nevertheless be measured. Chapter 3 asks you to consider whether assessment efforts could be focused on future performances instead of past ones. Chapter 4 asks you to consider whether naming, claiming, and protecting time for collaborative reflection on non-pressing matters could make your organization more effective. Together, those chapters set the stage for chapter 5, which asks you to consider the potential of making time for rubrics.

5

The Art of the Rubric

LET ME ACKNOWLEDGE that my readers with sensitive jargon-meters may be hearing loud beeping in their ears at this moment. *Rubric?* Others might be thinking, *Isn't that a cube?* No, that would be the Rubik's Cube, a popular 3-D puzzle. Actually, the word *rubric* has been around for a long time—deriving from the Middle English *rubike* (describing the red ocher pigments used in book headings) and from the Latin *rubrica* (also meaning *red*). But how the meaning morphed from color to assessment tool is somewhat of a mystery. One story is that the organizational associations with the word go back to the instructions written in red on a priest's copy of the liturgy, the words that literally told him *what to do next.*

In modern usage, *rubric* has various meanings: the heading of a part of a book or manuscript; the title of a statute; a category; an authoritative rule; an introductory explanatory commentary; an established rule or custom. You might feel that that's enough work for any one word to do, but let's add its common usage in the academic world: "a matrix that identifies criteria for success and describes levels of performance in relation to those criteria along a spectrum from poor to excellent."

Rubrics are ubiquitous in the world of education. Essays that are graded by multiple readers use rubrics to assure inter-rater reliability. Teachers use rubrics to grade student work. More important for our purposes, teachers use rubrics to help students understand what good work looks like *before they do it.* Rubrics help students understand what is expected of them. Here is one small example, from a Canadian educational website,[16] of a rubric on narrative writing. The full rubric lists criteria for various levels of performance in four areas: General Competence; Development; Mechanics; and finally Focus/Organization, which is excerpted in rubric 5.1.

Rubric 5.1: Narrative Analytic Rubric: Focus/Organization

Apprentice	Basic	Learned	Exemplary
Topic may not be clear. Few events are logical. May be no attempt to limit topic. Much digression or over-elaborations with significant interference with reader understanding.	Topic clear. Most events are logical. Some digression causing slight confusion. Most transitions are logical, but may be repetitive. Clear sense of beginning and end.	Topic clear. Events are logical. Possible slight digression without significant distraction to reader. Most transitions smooth and logical. Clear sense of beginning and end.	Topic clear. Events are logical. No digressions. Varied transitions. Transitions smooth and logical. Clear sense of beginning and end.

As they use this rubric with their teacher, students learn about concepts like *digressions* and *transitions*, and they begin to understand complex performances have multiple criteria for success.

Rubrics are not widely used in the social sector, and I believe they should be. To me, the rubric is a natural tool for a mission-driven organization. It provides a structure and format for asking what matters to us, and for describing what success will look like. It can be a vehicle for giving and receiving feedback because it provides the context for that feedback. It can literally *hold*, as in "contain," an ongoing conversation about what matters most to us while we tend to other urgent business. We create it in mission time, then it holds our thoughts for us until we can return again to that precious mission time. In other words, rubrics allow us to pick up right where we left off and avoid the age-old pitfalls of treading the same ground over and over in planning sessions and retreats. Used wisely, a rubric not only measures success, but also defines it and helps its users maintain momentum toward future plans and goals.

The beauty of the locally designed assessment rubric is that it is entirely yours. Its use is internal. It is self-designed and redesigned as needed, without worrying about strict criteria of validity or reliability, because its job is not to meet standards of scientific measurement—its job is to describe success. It can be, and most often is, *qualitative* not quantitative, because it is about what matters most to an organization. If it is not about something important, why create it?

I have had many conversations with social sector leaders who initially reject the very idea of measuring the things that matter most to them. "You can't measure that," they say, as if that is the end of the conversation. I remember attending an English department meeting early in my teaching career that had that end-of-conversation moment. The topic was how to build competency in writing throughout a four-year high school curriculum. When we began to identify criteria for success, the senior member of the department, an iconic figure with the obligatory tweed jacket, said, "I know good writing when I see it." Years later, I think that was fine for his legend but less helpful to his students, who spent their time trying to figure out what he wanted rather than following clear criteria for successful writing.

In more recent years, I remember the artistic director of a theater telling me no one could measure what mattered most to him. "What is that?" I asked. "The spiritual elevation of my audience," he answered. But then I asked him, "Can you describe it?" And the floodgates opened.

People are very good at describing what matters to them, because it's what they think about all the time. If you bring out a piece of paper at this point and say, "Let me write some of this down," you are on your way. The key is that you are about to use descriptive language to define various levels of quality, and it is these levels that become a scale for measuring what matters. The key to the rubric is getting both the topic and criteria right, then creating an actual spectrum of distinct levels of performance.

You may recall that in chapter 3 I recounted asking a series of questions in a board leadership workshop. The first was, *What would success look like in the next three to five years?* Questions 2 and 3 asked for more specifics. Question 4 asked what success would look like at an even higher level, and questions 5 and 6 asked for more specifics. This is the beginning of a rubric. If I had asked a third set of questions about what participants did *not* want to see—in other words, what would *disappoint* them in the next three to five years—each group would already have the raw material for a first draft of a rubric that would look something like what you see in rubric 5.2.

Rubric 5.2: Vision of Success for Your Organization in the Next 3–5 Years

Poor	Good	Excellent
The answers to the additional questions on what would be disappointing in the next 3–5 years, with an example.	The answers to questions 1, 2, and 3: what good success would look like in 3–5 years, with an example.	The answers to questions 4, 5 and 6: what exceptional success would look like in 3–5 years, with an example.

Perhaps between *poor* and *good*, we could add a column describing the status quo, with some minor improvements. From this preliminary rubric, we would likely extract certain criteria for success or areas to concentrate on and take it from there, writing new, more specific rubrics from scratch.

How do you write a rubric from scratch? Here is an exercise, which I first saw done by Jay McTighe, former director of the Maryland Assessment Consortium. I'll present it as if we were at a workshop together and add some commentary along the way. I invite you again to play along. It begins with people working individually.

— Getting Started: An Exercise —

Imagine you are the owner of a new restaurant. You are going to write a rubric that you will use to train your servers and give them feedback on the traits of their performance that matter most to you.

What would you do first? You know the rubric gives you the room to describe what you want to see and what you don't want to see. But in relation to what criteria? You can't describe everything. So you have to find a way to consider multiple criteria before you choose the most important ones.

Brainstorm possible traits, in the form of adjectives.

At this stage of rubric writing, it is important not to overthink and self-censor. Just make a list of possibilities. You know you will have to prioritize at some point, but for now let your imagination go. After a few minutes, you might have a list like this: friendly; attentive; knowledgeable; courteous; attractive; punctual; appropriately dressed; funny; dependable; coordinated; fast; honest; creative; unflappable.

Now choose four traits that matter enough to you that you will take the time to describe them along the spectrum represented across the rubric for 1 (low) to 4 (high).

At this point, you might have something like this:

	1	2	3	4
Knowledgeable·				
Courteous				
Witty				
Dependable				

The adjectives will be your own, and in choosing what to emphasize, you are already shaping what your restaurant will be known for. This is the first part of actual rubric writing: brainstorming and prioritizing criteria for success.

But have you noticed how easy it is so far? That's because you are doing it by yourself. What happens when you do this exercise with other people—which is, after all, the point of having assessment rubrics *for organizations*?

Sit down with your two new business partners, who conveniently enough have just done the same exercise you have. Decide *together* on the four words you will use for the servers' rubric at your new restaurant.

Aha! Unless you are unusually like-minded with your new partners, you will run into the challenge of synonyms. One of you said "attractive" while another said "well groomed." One of you said "attentive" while another said "punctual." One of you said "funny" while another said "witty." This part of the exercise illustrates two important points: (1) Words are important—you have to choose the ones you actually mean; and (2) organization-wide assessment requires conversations and consensus and sometimes compromise. The point is that you are getting on the same page regarding goals, standards, and criteria. You can't plan backward together effectively unless you do this. Not only are you doing your new servers a big favor by being clear about what you value and what you expect from them, you are also maximizing the prospects of harmony within your ownership team.

I would add here an observation prompted by this exercise: Without the discipline required by the rubric to be specific about what we are looking for, we can work side by side with colleagues for years operating like synonyms—headed in the same direction, but with slightly different trajectories. Think about your staff and board colleagues and ask if you all have the same definitions of why your organization exists and where you are headed.

Now choose one of the traits and describe what it would look like at an exemplary level (4), a high, perfectly acceptable level (3), a minimally acceptable level (2), and an unacceptable level (1).

For *dependable*, you might have something like:

	1	2	3	4
Dependable	Server is frequently late and occasionally does not show up for work	Server is occasionally late, but usually calls.	Server almost always shows up on time and always calls if running late.	Server always shows up on time.

The words you come up with are called descriptors in rubric lingo. There is nothing magic about the four levels—you could describe two, or eight. The point is to have enough shades of difference so that you help your servers improve without nitpicking over whether someone is a 6 or a 7 on a 9-point scale. That would be focusing unnecessary energy on the rubric, rather than focusing on the servers' performance. You will know you have good descriptors if several different people could watch the server over time and agree on the servers's current level of performance.

The conversations around descriptors inevitably raise important issues. You will agree that it is possible to be too attentive; that over-attentiveness should be described at the 1 or 2 level; and that your task in the box 4 is to describe the just-right level of attentiveness. Also, you can see how helpful it will be to describe bad behavior in the lowest box before it happens. You can head it off and prevent it rather than wait until someone needs to be chastised or corrected.

In real life, in real organizations, you would expand the circle of people drafting the rubric at this point. To use our example at hand, you would be crazy not to ask your new servers to build and refine the rubric. They will have knowledge and experience from previous jobs that will find their way into the rubric, and the servers will join you in defining and striving to perform good work. They will "own" it, which is every supervisor's dream.

But back to the exercise and a few more points about how rubrics can work for you. Let's imagine you have something like this now:

4	
Knowledgeable	The server knows the menu well, what is fresh today, and what the chef's specialties are; knows what wines will complement various dishes; has basic knowledge about what is going on in the city regarding theater.

Note this example includes at least one piece of knowledge that may not be immediately obvious—the information about what's going on in town. It is specific to this restaurant—we can see it is in a city and at least some of its clientele are from out of town. The planning-backward aspect of the rubric is very clear here. Now that you have identified something as desirable, it follows that there will be an organized approach to achieving it. It is hard to imagine a restaurant with this rubric for its servers not gathering them periodically to update knowledge in all these areas.

Part of the fun of a rubric comes at the next stage of construction:

Underneath the descriptive language you have used for each level of the rubric, add some indicators: specific examples of what we would see or hear at that level of performance.

Descriptors are meant to convey what is always true at that level of performance. Indicators may happen only once, but as examples, they help us understand what that level looks like. They breathe life into the descriptors. In a social profit organization, they will include the stories (at the top of the rubric) that best illustrate why that organization exists.

4

Knowledgeable	The server knows the menu well, what is fresh today, and what the chef's specialties are; knows what wines will complement various dishes; has basic knowledge about what is going on in the city regarding theater.
	• "Sir, I particularly recommend the duck. Chef Henri grew up in the Loire Valley, where they eat duck three meals a day."
	• "Yes, I have a recommendation for you. Do you enjoy musicals? We hear the revival of *Man of La Mancha* is getting standing ovations every night."

Now here is the best part and the reason I love rubrics. When they serve as a format for an ongoing discussion about good work, people pay attention to new and surprising indicators. Let's imagine you hear one of your servers say to a customer, "Good evening, Mr. Yingling. Welcome back." The server just raised the bar regarding what knowledge you would like to see your best servers have ready to use. You might add that sentence as a third indicator to the box above, but—even more important—you would *add to the descriptors*, as follows:

4

Knowledgeable	The server knows the menu well, what is fresh today, and what the chef's specialties are; knows what wines will complement various dishes; has basic knowledge about what is going on in the city regarding theater; and knows *the names of regular customers*.

This is how formative assessment works. It is not about hiring and firing servers. It is about having as much clarity and specificity as possible about what you are trying to do. It is about demystifying standards and criteria for success. It is about sharing the quest for excellence, not thinking it is the supervisor's job.

You can picture the servers at that restaurant gathered before opening and asking, now that the rubric includes this element, "Who are our regular customers?" And when somebody comes in that night and gets called by name, he starts to think, *This is my favorite restaurant.* Just as the LEED green building scale prompts someone to order local materials in order to meet LEED criteria, the server rubric helps servers plan to do what their employer values. The change in behavior is not because they are suddenly smarter, better, more empathetic people. It is because they are in an assessment system.

One final point. Any rubric can be a vehicle for helping organizations be more inclusive. Descriptions of good work can and should include the perspectives of clients. In this case, if I were the restaurant owner and my servers had a good rubric going, I'd gather a few of them and a small number of customers so we could ask the customers, "Are we missing anything?"

The server rubric is a simple example we can all relate to, and it suggests to us that the possible topics and uses of rubrics are endless. Sometimes I have to warn people not to become rubric-crazed. Rubrics take some time to write, and the pressing question becomes: What rubrics does your organization actually *need?* One organization in New Jersey, an arts group, responded to that question with an unexpected rubric (see rubric 5.3) that helps them do something quite basic but necessary: keep their workplace clean.

Obviously, the staff had some fun with this, and they added a feature our server rubric did not have—relative weighting of various criteria. You can see from the rubric that the state of the bathroom was an issue.

Rubric 5.3: Office Cleanliness

	1	2	3	4
Kitchen Area (25%)	Growth, nature encroaching	Dirty microwave, dirty fridge, food left out, spills	Coffee left in machine, clutter on countertop	No dirty dishes or utensils, no crumbs, Lysol-clean
Bathroom (30%)	Unusable	Dirty dishes, strong odors	Messy sink, dishes left out, no paper towels or toilet paper	Seat always down, clean sink and toilet, odor-free
Personal Space (10%)	Can't see computer screen through the dust, can't find chair because it is piled with clutter	Dusty, cluttered, unclean utensils and coffee mugs	Lunch left out, scattered papers	Dust-free computers and desktops, organized papers
Meeting Room (10%)	Space has become a storage area; no room to work	Food left on table, supplies not put back	Papers left out, objects not in proper place, paper cutter open	Pledge-clean, clear, rug vacuumed, no clutter
Front Office (25%)	Clutter every-where—looks like a bomb hit	Materials from closet not put away, stained carpet	Boxes left out, faxes strewn, mail scattered	No loose paper, no boxes, full candy jar

When I first saw this rubric, some weeks after our workshop, I asked the obvious question: *Does it work?* The answer, thankfully, was yes. The rubric, and the fun of making it, drew attention to the issues and let people talk about them at arm's length. The rubric was posted in the kitchen and bathroom, so instead of saying, "You left your food out again and didn't clean up that spill," people had the option of saying, "I think I see a 2 coming on. Two alert!" The whole place was cleaner. A year later, though, I met some employees from the same organization. I asked them if they knew the rubric, and they were puzzled. I asked if their office was clean, and they said, "Not really." The writers of the rubric had moved on and left the rubric on the wall, but not the thinking behind it. The moral of this story is that good assessment is ongoing. (Here's a surprise ending: I recently saw yet another group of new employees at the same organization, and they told me they use the rubric all the time!)

Formative assessment can have some practical applications like this one on office cleanliness, but more typically it involves writing rubrics that get at the core purpose of an organization. We ask what it would look like to succeed in our mission, goals, and strategies. We ask if there is something that matters a lot to us that resists quantification. We ask if there is something we need to talk about that we haven't found a way to talk about yet. We ask if there is a key performance in the work of our organization, one that would benefit from being described more specifically so that people can get better at it. We ask if there is an essential question to our work, one we never get to the end of, where we need a vehicle for ongoing discussion and learning. We ask what is the social profit we are trying to bring about.

Rubrics can help us respond to these questions over time and get more and more precise in our answers. So carve out some mission time and give it a try. The next chapter supports that effort.

6

Practical Advice on Rubric Design

If a joke sticks around for generations, it must be ringing true. Such is the case with the one about the tourist walking the streets in New York City who calls out to a cabdriver for directions: "How do I get to Carnegie Hall?" The cabbie yells back: "Practice!" That's just the advice I would give to you if after having read the preceding chapters you are tempted to share this approach with colleagues and to write some assessment rubrics yourselves. As you shift from thinking about formative assessment on a theoretical level to actually trying it, I will shift from teacher to coach and offer the following practical advice, based on experience, and beginning with the punch line of the old joke.

—— Developing Any Skill ——
Takes Practice

It is rare that groups write rubrics together effortlessly right away. Regrettably, I have seen groups give it a try, run into a snag or get frustrated over a colleague's reluctance to participate, or a disagreement over words, and then simply give up. If they have not identified mission time for ongoing work, that's the end of it. There are plenty of urgent tasks in front of them that they already know how to do.

But even with mission time set aside, people can become discouraged if rubric writing and group decision making do not come quickly or easily enough to satisfy those who are itching to get back to the work piling up on their desks. It is helpful to think about the whole process as a skill, like learning a new language. Skills take practice. Practice requires patience. You can remain patient if you have faith that practice will pay off.

The comparison to learning a language is instructive when applied to a group. It may not be the language you traditionally use together, but you may find some members of the group already know it. Others pick up new languages very quickly. Some struggle. The same range in speed of adaptation will be seen in a group embracing the ideas of formative assessment, rubric writing, and self-assessment. It is important to know that with patience, over time, everyone will be speaking the same language. But remember that busy people in busy organizations do not have time to practice, especially to practice *together*, unless time is set aside for the purpose.

— Don't Write Rubrics Alone —

Several years ago, about a week after a rubric workshop, I received a fully developed rubric via email that seemed almost perfect to me. It was from an organization that partnered with universities, and it laid out the various dimensions of the relationship and described what the two partners needed from each other to make the program work, as well as what it looked like when those elements were missing. It was clear, specific, and immediately understandable. I was feeling happy for them and inordinately proud of myself as their teacher.

Then a few days later, I bumped into the executive director of that organization and complimented him on the rubric. "What rubric?" he said. His young associate had gone home and written the rubric herself. No one else had seen it yet. The rubric could still eventually be helpful, but she had missed the chance to bring others into its creation and therefore "own" it. If I had *really* been an effective teacher that day, I would have urged her to write her rubric to get a feel for the territory, then erase everything except the title and some suggested criteria and then ask her colleagues to work on it with her.

It is tempting to write a rubric alone for obvious reasons— you can get it done quickly, and you can avoid disagreement and conflict. But if someone hands you a completed rubric, it feels like a message from that person that you are supposed to work harder or better. It feels like, "Here's what I want you to do." Regarding our natural inclination to avoid conflict, we have to remember that *part of the purpose of the rubric is to provide a format and process for working things out.* You will be working out things that matter, or else why would you be writing a rubric about them?

— Write DRAFT at the Top —

The simple word DRAFT signals an atmosphere of ongoing learning and reminds you that the rubric is holding a conversation you will return to as you learn from experience and the world changes around you. It also allows you to share the rubric with others in ever-widening circles, not as a finished document but as an inquiry. Each draft represents the *best thinking so far* of the group that has been creating it.

— Allow One Rubric to Lead to Another —

Rubrics have a habit of guiding you to what you most need to talk about. You might begin with an organization-wide scan of all your constituents, and that might bring up discussion of, say, your board. Then the narrowed focus might take you to what's actually been bothering you—that board members don't seem to be doing anything between meetings, for instance. The ensuing discussion may lead you to clear understandings not only about what board members can and should be doing in a number of areas but also about what the executive director or other staff need to do to support them.

In short, don't feel you have to finish a rubric just because you started it. If something more compelling emerges, follow it. Remember that the rubric is not the point; creating social value is the point. Your touchstone should be, *Will working on this rubric eventually improve our work, and/or our ability and capacity to do it?*

— Don't Forget About Indicators — and Other Ways to Personalize

I am arguing that organizations should take assessment into their own hands. One way to do that is to include indicators in your rubrics that invoke personalities and well-known events and stories unique to your organization. Rather than using numbers to define a spectrum of performance, describe the levels with your own terminology. Let's say that Mary, the now-deceased founder of a social service agency, had been especially noted for her warmth and empathy for her clients. If her successors were writing a rubric titled "Client Service," they might choose to name the next-to-highest level "Mary is smiling" and the top of the rubric "Mary is cheering." The bottom of the rubric, the behavior they want to avoid, might be labeled, "Mary comes back to haunt us."

The boxes in a rubric expand as you fill them, so don't be shy about including your favorite stories and organizational legends.

Imagine, for example, that an environmental organization has created a rubric on "Communication," and one of the criteria for success is "outreach to a wider audience." At the top of the rubric in this row, the group might include something like "Jake's letter in the *Times* on Earth Day 2005." Technology being what it is, they could insert a photograph of a beaming Jake holding a copy of the newspaper right into the rubric.

Or at the other end of the spectrum, let's take something that actually happened to me, not one of my proudest moments. I was conducting a Dodge Foundation site visit at Two River Theater in Red Bank, New Jersey, and I showed up completely unexpectedly. Despite my protests, the managing director was roused from his home where he was enjoying a quiet day off. In our rubric on site visits (see rubric 7.6 in the next chapter), that incident would fall in the "unacceptable" column and deserves its own shorthand like "Two-River-gate." (Needless to say, it is good practice to nominate others for the upper ends of the rubrics and yourself for the lower ends when you deserve it.)

— Don't Feel You Need a — Whole Rubric Every Time

Some rubrics need to be fleshed out along the whole spectrum of performance, because it is helpful to be specific about what *not* to do as well as what performance looks like at the top. Some don't. I worked with an organization that began to write a full rubric on the performance of volunteers and then decided to turn it into a simple matrix that identified areas of performance, from attending meetings to making connections in the community, and then described "best practice" in each area. No spectrum—just suggestions of what is appreciated and valued.

— Take the Rubric —
Out for a Test Drive

You learn a lot about how a rubric can serve you by trying it out. Take whatever number draft you have and use it to prioritize your actions and, at the appropriate time, to evaluate your performance. You will almost always find that something is missing, or something needs to be stated more clearly or specifically. Then go back and create the next draft and decide what you will do differently as a result.

— Once You Get the Hang of It, —
Invite Others In

Rubrics are about better performance in the long run, and better performance can come from more inclusive processes. The rubric is a natural vehicle for inclusiveness because the word DRAFT indicates it can always be improved with new insights and perspectives. It will be particularly helpful to have the people you serve take a look at rubrics that describe levels of service and ask, "What are we missing?" and "Would you help us improve this?"

My favorite story of inviting others in was when the program officers at the Dodge Foundation were writing a rubric about their jobs. They described performance in relation to the criteria that occurred to them first: keeping up with the field; interacting with grantees; being innovative in making connections. Then they invited the program assistants at the home office to look at the rubric, and almost as a group, they responded, "What about *being organized?*" Consider this a design principle: *If other people are in your rubric, invite them to help you write it.* (See rubric 7.3 for a cautionary tale on this topic.)

— Don't Forget About —
Mission Time

Not making time for this work is the single biggest mistake you can make. Have I emphasized this enough? Probably not. Mission time does not have to be in the form of a retreat. A relatively easy way to start is to use existing meeting time and simply designate the last ten or fifteen minutes of a staff meeting as mission time. There will be resistance, which I will address in chapter 10 on managing change. But you can have quick victories that will help make the case for both mission time and the formative assessment approach.

Do a quick SWOT exercise one week, discuss it the next, and make a clear change the next, addressing a widely recognized weakness, or seizing an opportunity of the low-hanging-fruit variety. Or you can ask in a short meeting, *Do you think we are doing a good job of measuring what matters most to us?* This will evoke the *You can't measure that* response, but you know what to say: *Then let's try to describe it.* The conversation will begin, and you can bring out the rubric later, if you choose.

As the benefits of regular mission time become apparent, you may want to separate it from a weekly staff meeting that must necessarily deal with matters that are more urgent. When my wife and I were starting a new school in the early 1980s with the help of very smart colleagues, we fell into the pattern of two weekly faculty meetings. One was about which students were having trouble and needed our attention, what operational details we had forgotten, and who was driving the van to town on Saturday. The second meeting was about long-term matters: our sense of what was working and not working as we tried various activities, our "picture of the graduate" from which we could plan backward as we designed the educational program, and our vision for the future in terms of facilities, staffing needs, and key relationships.

I have been focusing on mission time for staff, because board members already have the benefit of mission time if their meetings are well conceived and well run. Board meetings are infrequent compared with staff meetings. Sometimes they are monthly; often they are quarterly. Thus it is essential that they be about the big-picture health and direction of the organization and not be cluttered with reports that could have been handled in other ways, though many board meetings have exactly that problem. Board meetings that focus on a series of self-assessment questions tend to be more enjoyable and productive: *Are we clear about the difference we want to make in the world? How will we know if we are being successful? How is the world changing around us, and what difference does that make to our strategies? Are we keeping our organization healthy and capable of performing at the level to which we aspire?*

— Learn from Other Organizations —

There are some basic tasks where simple rubrics would apply across the sector: building a strong board; managing a leadership transition; planning and executing a capital campaign. With rubrics in these areas, it is useful to see how other organizations adapt accepted practice to fit their own cultures and circumstances. One of the rubrics in the next chapter, on site visits by foundation officers, falls in this category and could be modified by any grantmaking organization.

Most of the examples in the next three chapters, though, are more customized self-assessment tools, invented by a range of social profit organizations in different fields and geographic locations to serve their core purposes. Each rubric has a story to tell, and I hope you and your colleagues will consider how to adapt their lessons to your own situation. It may be useful to ask, "What would be our equivalent?

7

Rubrics That Improve Performance

LET'S LOOK AT SOME STORIES of the creation and use of rubrics by different types and sizes of organizations. The rubrics have different purposes, from training neighborhood leaders to capturing the multiple dimensions of "greening" religious institutions. In each case, I will present full organizational rubrics and offer some commentary referring to specific parts. The creators of each rubric have also weighed in with some thoughts about lessons learned.

The point I hope you take away from this chapter is that rubrics can focus attention and change behavior in desirable ways. They can help you produce social profit directly, recognize weaknesses that are holding you back, and strengthen your organization in ways that result in further social profit.

A Community Foundation Trains Its Fellows: The Neighborhood Leadership Initiative Training Rubric

From 1991 to 2006, the Community Foundation of New Jersey (CFNJ) offered training to selected fellows to help them create and implement projects that would benefit their communities—usually urban neighborhoods. Called the Neighborhood Leadership Initiative (NLI), these training sessions were already well established and well regarded before the program directors discovered rubrics in 2000. What makes this story particularly compelling to me is that then, by all accounts, the program got better.

The program directors, Ira Resnick and Faith Krueger, worked with fellows to create the following framework for the NLI rubric, which you will notice right away is practically a narrative of the steps required for each project to be successful. As rubric 7.1 shows, the rubric's nine rows unfold sequentially, reflecting each stage of the project, and the columns describe at what level the leader engages others during each stage.

Rubric 7.1: The Template for the NLI Training Rubric

Organizing Process	Alone	Circle of Friends	Cooperation	Partnership
Vision				
Preparing a Case Statement				
Asset Mapping				
Mobilizing a Leadership Team				
Prioritize Goals				
Program Design				
Program Implementation				
Celebration				
Evaluation				

The basic template names a series of steps and makes the space to describe how to do them well (and not so well). It also uses well-chosen words instead of numbers to define levels of performance in relation to the level of community buy-in and participation the leader achieves. The column heads describe a spectrum from a leader working alone, to a leader working in actual partnership with the community involved, and these headings announce the core value of this particular leadership program.

The people behind NLI were not interested in the heroic loner who made something happen through dint of individual effort; they were interested in building neighborhood connections that would last beyond any particular project. Ira and Faith explained to me that simply having these headings in the rubric enabled them to have a conversation that had eluded them for years—about the difference between the *activist* and the *leader*. In the NLI rubric, the person who takes charge and moves ahead with little or no community building gets the lowest rating. Rubric 7.2 shows the first third of the completed rubric and reflects both the tasks and the values of a well-led NLI project.

I appreciate the fact that the next-to-highest level on the rubric, the one called "Cooperation," is so ambitious in its expectations. For example, in the early stages of the process, we see descriptions at this level as follows:

For "Vision": Leader has clear vision and goals, demonstrates the ability to describe concrete, achievable goals. Leader possesses effective oral and written communication skills to convey his/her story.

For "Asset Mapping": Leader is familiar with asset-based approach to community development. Has working knowledge of public and private institutions, organizations, and agencies in the neighborhood. Creates an asset map that includes significant networks within the neighborhood.

In both cases, we may be tempted to say, "That sounds pretty good." In the absence of the rubric, if I saw that level of performance, I am not sure I would make any critique at all. But then the

Rubric 7.2: NLI Organizing Process for Successful Community Initiatives

Organizing Process	Alone	Circle of Friends	Cooperation	Partnership
Vision	Leader lacks ability to communicate vision or story clearly with others.	Leader can present some parts of a compelling story. Story lacks purpose or impact for change.	Leader has a clear vision and goals, demonstrates the ability to describe concrete, achievable goals. Leader possesses effective oral and written communication skills to convey his/her story.	Leader demonstrates the skill to establish relationships with listeners, creates shared vision of potential community change based upon mutual goals and values.
Preparing a Case Statement	Leader verbally presents a vague goal without additional information.	Leader prepares a sentence that includes a goal and supporting evidence about the need to accomplish the proposed project's goal. Leader may discuss the case statement with a friend or two.	Leader prepares a written case statement that includes a specific goal, with some parts of the balance of a case statement. Leader distributes case statement to interested local leaders.	Leader prepares a written paragraph that includes: goal, potential stakeholders, strategy, and proposed outcomes. Leader "tests" case statement with local leaders and makes appropriate revisions.
Asset Mapping	Leader is unable to identify assets in his/her community. Sees only deficiencies and needs.	Leader identifies a limited number of neighborhood assets that reflect his/her own personal network of acquaintances and friends.	Leader is familiar with asset-based approach to community development. Has a working knowledge of public and private institutions, organizations, and agencies in the neighborhood. Creates an asset map that includes significant networks within the neighborhood.	Leader constructs an asset map that includes institutions, agencies, and organizations that impact upon his/her community. Conducts one-on-one meetings that establish relationships with stakeholders and potential new allies to change community conditions.

rubric describes an even higher level, the top of the rubric, called "Partnership":

For "Vision": Leader demonstrates the skill to establish relationships with listeners, creates shared vision of potential community change based upon mutual goals and visions.

For "Asset Mapping": Leader constructs an asset map that includes institutions, agencies, and organizations that impact his/her community. Conducts one-on-one meetings that establish relationships with stakeholders and potential new allies to change community conditions.

This is like the LEED scale helping me understand why I should buy local or regional materials for a green building, or the server rubric helping me realize I should learn the names of regular customers. Now that I know what it "looks like" to do work at the highest levels, I can proceed to do it, or at least try. The NLI fellows who scheduled those one-on-one meetings were not suddenly smarter, better people; they had an assessment tool.

The concept of planning backward permeates this rubric. The eighth row is labeled "Celebration." The NLI fellows read the following *before their projects begin* about what performance looks like at the highest level, "Partnership":

For "Celebration": Leader arranges community-wide event to recognize and salute the stakeholders within the community whose shared vision and commitment have made possible the change taking place.

Now, there's something to plan backward from! It would be impossible to accomplish this without working toward the shared vision to begin with, as described in the first row of the rubric. And knowing the event will be important, everyone saves the date well in advance rather than having the leader ask, "Can you make it to a celebration next weekend?"

Because Ira and Faith developed this rubric with several years of fellows, it became widely "owned." I asked whether the rubric was improving the work. Ira said, "In the first seven or eight years of the program, before we developed the rubric, I would say we had four or five projects I would have rated at the top. In this year alone, now that we are using it, I would say over half of the projects, maybe a dozen, reached that standard." Again, it was not that they had a sudden influx of skilled community organizers. They had a rubric.

As we all know, grassroots projects in challenged neighborhoods take an abundance of sweat equity and patience. We used the rubric with our grassroots community leaders as they began to plan their neighborhood projects to help them envision the possibilities and potentials [talents] of the various partners that would be required to make the project a success. It was imperative that there was a true, genuine consensus among identified local community leaders that the need for the project or program was real. Equally important, we used the rubric to show them that if they had a successful project, all along they would have been cultivating a string of upcoming leaders for program sustainability. We strongly believed that participating in the project would further strengthen community ownership, as well as shield the leader from "burnout" or possession issues.

Faith Krueger, chief operating officer,
Community Foundation of New Jersey

— An Attempt to Help Social Workers — and Physicians Integrate Patient Care: The Community Care for Depression Rubric

When the Robert Wood Johnson Foundation's Local Funding Partnerships Program asked me to meet with their grantees to talk about assessment, I saw firsthand that I did not have to know anything about the organization's field to be helpful. A consortium of health care agencies from Cape Cod was together integrating the work of behavioral health specialists with that of primary care providers (PCPs) to serve patients suffering from depression.

The project director came to my assessment workshop. He had never heard of a rubric, but he went back to his office and assembled a group to write a rubric on what integrated teamwork would look like. Eventually, in the way they defined the spectrum of performance, they created a rubric that, like the NLI's, announces a value and an intention to act on that value. Here are their column heads, describing the various levels at which practitioners from the two fields worked together:

Bifurcated, split, at odds	Parallel: in the same building, paths cross but limited teamwork	Getting together . . . getting there . . . getting to know you!	Integrated: team works together seamlessly

The rows in the rubric reflect various concerns—from medical records, protocols, and space needs to personnel issues and quality of care. Their working draft, shown in rubric 7.3, clearly lays out what success looks like in each of these areas at each level of cooperation—from working at odds to working together seamlessly. (The acronym *EMR* stands for "electronic medical record.")

Rubric 7.3: Community Care for Depression Rubric for Integration of Behavioral Health and Primary Care

	Bifurcated, split, at odds	Parallel: in the same building, paths cross but limited teamwork
EMR/Medical Records	PCPs don't read behavioral health notes or actively seek behavioral health information about patients. Social workers don't read provider notes or seek medical information. EMRs are set up so that interdisciplinary access to notes is difficult or impractical.	PCPs and social workers are aware that the information is available to them but not at the point where they find it necessary to review.
Space	Medical and behavior health disciplines rarely cross paths formally or informally because of office structures, separate floors, etc. Behavioral health is rigid about the 50-minute hour, no interruptions, etc. PCPs lack understanding of time necessary for counselors to deal with behavioral health complexities.	Medical and behavioral health providers try to check in with one another but it is difficult because they are not able to track one another down.
Materials	Primary care and behavioral health information doesn't cross disciplines; is not shared across lines. Disciplines don't see each other's information as relevant to what they do.	PCPs occasionally give out behavioral health brochures if they happen to have them available.
Processes/ Protocols	Behavioral health protocols are not understood/applied by providers. Primary care protocols aren't understood by behavioral health. There are no interdisciplinary meetings. Case review doesn't happen, or happens separately.	PCPs and social workers occasionally chat about extremely complicated patients.
Personnel	Medical and behavioral health staff don't know one another. Team members are unaware of one another's disciplines, stressors, and why they entered their chosen profession. Burnout can be a significant factor in both disciplines, particularly so when, because of bifurcation, there is limited teamwork.	Behavioral and medical staff have a limited knowledge of other staff, and occasionally cross paths, but don't have time to go beyond initial pleasantries and introductions.

DRAFT

Getting together . . . getting there . . . getting to know you!	Integrated: team works together seamlessly
PCPs and social workers begin to look further into the EMR and take all notes into consideration when seeing the patient.	EMR system is utilized regularly in a way that consistently tracks both the medical and behavioral health of each patient (pop-ups, etc.). Both disciplines read notes and respond accordingly. The EMR is set up so that interdisciplinary access is seamless. Any acute or emergent information is easily communicated to relevant staff.
PCPs and social workers make it a point to check in with one another regularly on particular patients. Offices are located as near as possible to one another. Each discipline welcomes visits from the other.	Counseling and exam rooms are situated so that social workers and PCPs can easily check in and compare patient information during the day. Administration supports co-location of offices and disciplines.
PCPs and behavioral health providers have a variety of materials to hand out to patients, stressing the importance of both fields of treatment.	PCPs and social workers embrace the need to look at patients from a "whole person" perspective and encourage patients to see their health in the same manner by distributing materials to that effect.
PCPs and social workers make an effort to spend more time comparing notes and looking for ways to work together for the benefit of the patient.	Social workers and PCPs understand that they are both integral parts of a patient's "whole" care. They meet regularly as a team in order to discuss patients and handle issues as a joint intervention.
Behavioral health and medical staff make an effort to meet occasionally to get to know one another.	Social workers and PCPs attend a regular roundtable meeting. They get to know one another on a personal level and begin to understand the motivating factors of the other's professions. This knowledge translates to more teamwork and mutual support.

Rubric 7.3 (continued)

	Bifurcated, split, at odds	Parallel: in the same building, paths cross but limited teamwork
Attitudes Toward Patients	PCPs not always aware or interested in the stressors that affect the lives of the underprivileged. The providers' schedules are tight, and patients are expected to keep their appointments. When stressed, staff and all disciplines may blame the patient when problems arise.	PCPs are aware that there may be non-compliant patients but tend to blame no-shows on the social worker.
Focus of Treatment	Since behavioral health does not generate as much revenue as medical care, it is not considered as important. Behavioral health is perceived as adjunct to primary care rather than complementary.	The accent is on the medical model for PCP; patients are referred to behavioral health, and behavioral health focuses on related issues except where there is a clear medical issue.
Quality vs. Quantity of Care	Number and length of visits is driven by reimbursement concerns.	A few patients are given more than 15- to 30-minute visits, but this occurs only rarely.
Understanding of Our Mission	Organizational mission statements are either unknown to staff or viewed as an abstraction—words that aren't relevant to patient care.	Mission statements are known but not well understood or not viewed as applicable to patient care and the performance of duties.

In this rubric, rather than focus on a series of actions, the creators focused on conditions and context, describing success in areas as specific as medical records and as broad as mission comprehension. My two favorite rows illustrate how a rubric can take you to the areas that most need attention. For the criteria of "Space," the difference between where they were starting and where they wanted to go was stark:

At the "Bifurcated" level: Medical and behavioral health disciplines rarely cross paths formally or informally because of office structures/separate floors, etc.

Getting together . . . getting there . . . getting to know you!	Integrated: team works together seamlessly
PCPs understand that it can be difficult for patients to keep an appointment if they don't have a vehicle or are unable to miss a day of work. Accommodations are made.	PCPs have a deeper sense of the issues facing the underprivileged: homelessness, lack of transportation, socioeconomic factors, language barriers, and cultural differences. All disciplines are trained to do brief motivational assessments before suggesting interventions to patients.
Each discipline recognizes the value of integration to health outcomes. Interest in learning from one another increases, and teamwork becomes more common.	A patient is seen as a whole person and care of the mind and body are equally important. Interventions are responded to jointly, rather than seen as the responsibility of one discipline or the other. There is consistency. All disciplines are valued and seen as vital to the care of the patient.
It is recognized that some clients need extra time, so modifications are made for complex needs (e.g., mental illness and language barriers).	Primary care and behavioral health visits are of sufficient length to reasonably respond to patient needs.
Mission statements are known and understood. Staff have an increasing awareness that integration relates to the overall mission of the community health center because it improves quality of care.	Mission statements are known and understood as relevant to patient care. Staff understand that integration of PC and BH is in the best interest of the clients, as it improves health outcomes. Administration supports integration and regularly stresses its importance to all staff and new hires.

At the "Integrated" level: Counseling and exam rooms are situated so that social workers and PCPs can easily check in and compare patient information during the day. Administration supports co-location of offices and disciplines.

Here is a reminder that the physical environment both encourages and limits certain kinds of behavior. If you have a clear picture of what you are trying to accomplish and your space is working against you, you change the space. Similarly, the Community Care for Depression project team used the rubric to identify another factor that was holding them back, in the row for "Personnel":

At the "Bifurcated" level: Behavioral health and medical staff don't know one another. Team members are unaware of one another's disciplines, stressors, and why they entered their chosen profession.

At the "Integrated" level: Social workers and PCPs attend a regular roundtable meeting. They get to know one another on a personal level and begin to understand the motivating factors of the other's profession.

One thing I discovered about behavioral health integration into primary care practices is, "It don't come easy." The idea, obvious to me anyway, that we treat people holistically, is often scoffed at. We used the rubric in various ways but mostly to describe what integration was and where we would like it to be at the four community health centers involved, all staffed/housed differently and serving different patient populations. We held monthly meetings with project staff and compared progress/digressions using the rubric as our measuring stick. We did not include primary care physicians in the writing of the rubric, because it was much easier for me to assemble the team of four social workers I managed. Looking back, if we had, I think the rubric would have been that much better. I would have included primary care physicians, case managers, and anyone else who could have added perspective. It would have also been great to include the CEO or even board members.

Tim Lineaweaver, Quissett Counseling and Consulting,
former project director,
Community Care for Depression

If knowing one another better will be better for you and your patients, you figure out a way to make that happen. There is an important point here about why organizations need to organize and elevate the practice of measuring what matters. There is little doubt that individuals, including the project director, had noticed that these matters needed attention. But noticing things does not mean things will change. The odds for change vastly increase when there is a process that *prioritizes* what matters and paints a picture of the way things should be. Because it is an internal process, it carries internal authority, and the more inclusive the process is, the more powerful that authority will be.

As much as I admire this rubric, I also see it as a cautionary tale. When you read through the rubric you are struck by the fact that it is written from the point of view of the social workers. It undoubtedly clarified the challenges of integrating patient care for them, but it did not necessarily bring about that integration— *because the primary care providers weren't in on it.* I now offer the following principle when I am coaching organizations on rubric design: *If other people are in your rubric, invite them to help you write it.* In retrospect, the project director's one regret was not including all parties in the creation of the rubric.

Setting Goals for Environmental Stewardship: The GreenFaith Assessment Rubric for Religious Institutions

GreenFaith is a faith-based environmental organization whose mission is to "inspire, educate and mobilize people of diverse religious backgrounds for environmental leadership." Their leaders created a comprehensive rubric that helped them see how far "greening" could go beyond solar panels on the roof of a church, recycling at a synagogue, or a high-efficiency furnace at a mosque. They decided to describe performance in seven areas of institutional life: worship and spirituality; religious education; fellowship and social life; facility management; social outreach; financial management; and influence on members, denominations, and community.

For the spectrum of performance, they had some fun with religious imagery, but they also suggested that moving to a high level of environmental responsibility and leadership is a spiritual journey:

Out of the Garden	In the Wilderness	Building a New Ark	Eden Restored

As you read the result, rubric 7.4, you will have your own favorite parts. I like the awareness of how important it is to have board-level policies that will require certain behaviors and decisions, such as those for green facility management and for investments, and I like the call for connections to nonreligious partners such as providers of local food and regional environmental organizations.

This rubric is about both mind-set and practice. In the area of religious education, what a difference between the bottom and top of the rubric! At the lowest level, "Out of the Garden," we read, "Members [are] taught that God is found only through sacred texts." At the highest level, "Eden Restored," by contrast, "Adult, teenage, [and] youth members [are] taught that [the] natural world is a revelatory gift." Here is a debate with religious, historical, philosophical, cultural, and psychological implications in one row of a rubric.

And once again, I am struck by how the rubric can take an admirable level of performance and invite you to strive for more. If you had asked me what green worship looked like, I would have thought the following would more than suffice:

Worship and Spirituality at the "Building a New Ark" level (next to highest): Monthly positive, compassionate references to natural world in worship, sermons, teaching. Eco-theological references address at least two dimensions of eco-theological concern (spirit, stewardship, justice). Prayers offer thanks and call for repentance in relation to the earth. Plants and animals welcomed into services at least once a year. At least two services held outdoors each year. Members encouraged to seek the spirit in nature and taught basic techniques. At least one eco-service annually given second-tier holy-day significance.

But the rubric imagined a higher level:

Worship and Spirituality at the "Eden Restored" level (highest): Several sermons a year focus on eco-themes. Eco-examples figure in many other sermons. Mature eco-theology includes references to spirit, stewardship, justice. Outdoor worship each season; series of creation observances yearly. Prayers weekly reference the earth and beyond-human forms of life. Plants and animals—particularly local species—welcomed into worship at least four times a year. Members taught eco-spiritual practice. At least one service annually given holy-day significance.

When I asked GreenFaith's executive director, the Reverend Fletcher Harper, what effect this multipart visioning had on the institutions he worked with, he said it was essential, because it directly confronted "the initial confusion, or the fragmented nature of the vision" of congregations and schools for whom the environment was not a top-tier priority. He explained, "If we wanted to elevate the environment's importance for them, we needed to find a way to lay out a broad, comprehensive, attractive picture of what we wanted their future to look like. The rubric was the best way we found to do that."

Rubric 7.4: GreenFaith Rubric for Religious Institutions

Area of Institutional Life	Out of the Garden	In the Wilderness
1. Worship & Spirituality • Worship • Sermons • Spiritual practices	No reference or derogatory references are made to the earth in prayers and/or sermons. Plants/animals never integrated into worship services. Members are discouraged from environment-based spiritual practices. No worship services held outdoors.	Positive, compassionate references to God's creation of the natural world in sermons and prayers on environmentally oriented feast days or near Earth Day. Eco-theology addresses nature in only one dimension—spiritual/stewardship/justice—but not further developed. Recognition in sermons/teaching that people can seek/encounter the divine in nature, without any explicit encouragement or techniques to do so. Flowers integrated into worship space without regard to season, locality. One worship service/year held wholly/partly outdoors.
2. Religious Education • Children • Teens • Adults • Biblical • Theological • Ethical • Personal experiences	Members taught that God is found only through sacred texts. Teaching refers to natural world as fallen/sinful, not part of ultimate salvation/paradise. Members taught explicitly or by exclusion that religion focuses only on the divine–human relationship. No reference made to human responsibility for creation. No opportunities for direct contact with natural world as part of education programming.	Members in only one age group taught that the natural world is a revelatory gift. Teaching does not refer to natural world as sinful/fallen; creation not discussed in relation to salvation/paradise. Teaching suggests that religion focuses on well-being of all creation. Reference made once–twice annually to human responsibility for creation. Outdoors referenced.
3. Fellowship and Social Life • Food • Cutlery/plates • Training for home	No thought given to environmental impact of food consumption or fellowship-related supplies; cost is only consideration.	Food shifted to fruit/vegetables on at least 30% of congregational fellowship events; one event sourced locally/sustainably/fair trade.

Building a New Ark	Eden Restored
Monthly positive, compassionate references to natural world in worship, sermons, teaching.	Several sermons a year focus on eco-themes. Eco-examples figure in many other sermons.
Eco-theological references address at least two dimensions of eco-theological concern (spirit, stewardship, justice).	Mature eco-theology includes references to spirit, stewardship, justice.
Prayers offer thanks and call for repentance in relation to the earth.	Outdoor worship each season; series of creation observances yearly.
Plants and animals welcomed into services at least once a year.	Prayers weekly reference the earth and beyond-human forms of life.
At least two services held outdoors each year.	Plants and animals—particularly local species—welcomed into worship at least four times a year.
Members encouraged to seek the spirit in nature and taught basic techniques.	Members taught eco-spiritual practices.
At least one eco-service annually given second-tier holy-day significance.	At least one service annually given holy-day significance.
Members in two age groups taught that natural world is a revelatory gift; at least one age group taught that humanity has responsibility for environmental care.	Adult, teenage, youth members taught that natural world is a revelatory gift; adults and teens taught that humanity has responsibility for environmental care.
At least three weeks of educational programming/year for each of two age groups, addressing biblical, ethical, theological themes.	Education teaches eco-theology, biblical, ethical, and environment-based spiritual practices.
Creation included within the openly acknowledged moral universe of the congregation, and included in the community that is ultimately saved/redeemed.	Members of all ages given opportunities for direct contact with/service to nature, with opportunities for reflection and prayer.
	Members encouraged to recall spiritual experiences in nature, to develop spiritual and moral maturity in relation to nature.
Food for events sourced locally/sustainably/fair trade for at least 25% of the year; cutlery/plates/dishwasher replace disposables.	Food for events sourced locally/sustainably/fair trade; members encouraged three times a year to reduce food footprint; all cutlery and plates washed in dishwasher.

Rubric 7.4 (continued)

Area of Institutional Life	Out of the Garden	In the Wilderness
4. Facility Management • Energy conservation • Renewable energy • Water • Waste • Toxics • Training for home	No effort made in any area.	Initial efforts made in energy conservation, though congregation remains dependent on outside organizations for follow-up and accountability.
5. Social Outreach • Volunteer activities • Financial giving • Advocacy	No care for the earth expressed through social outreach and justice activities; programming supported that inadvertently or openly uses natural resources in unsustainable ways	Care for the earth affirmed as a religious value; activity in one of the three areas of financial/volunteer/advocacy commitments. Activity linked to major feast day or Earth Day.
6. Financial Management • Endowment/ reserve fund management • Modeling for members	No care for earth expressed through financial management. Financial profit only consideration.	At least 30% of investment portfolio environmentally screened.
7. Influence on Members, Denomination, Community	No effort made to influence behavior of members, denomination, and community.	Passive support given for greening initiatives in community/denomination and among members. Congregation does not initiate efforts to influence these areas.

Building a New Ark	Eden Restored
Efforts made in at least two areas of facility management; reporting system organized for governing board. Governing board affirms green facility management as a goal.	Efforts made in all areas of facility management, supported by organizational policies and training. Members encouraged to implement these practices at home and provided with training and tools to accomplish this.
Care for the earth affirmed as a religious value; activity in two of the three areas of financial/volunteer/advocacy commitments. Advocacy commitment of some kind undertaken at least once annually.	Care for the earth affirmed as a value equal in importance to other moral priorities. Volunteer opportunities, financial commitments, advocacy commitments fostered and encouraged for all age groups. Regular outreach habits in relation to the earth—akin to monthly food donations—put into practice. Active partnerships with regional environmental groups and beyond. Congregation invests time and resources in struggles for concrete environmental improvements on behalf of at-risk communities.
Environmentally screened investment portfolio.	Environmentally screened investment portfolio; actively votes shareholder proxies for the environment; encourages members to do the same.
Congregation initiates efforts to influence own members' behavior and supports others' initiatives to influence community/denomination.	Congregation initiates efforts to influence members, community, denomination, and is known as a leader in each of these areas.

When a thoughtful rubric defines and clarifies standards, it can be applied in ever-widening circles and with more and more authority. The rubric above evolved into the GreenFaith Certification Program, a two-year environmental leadership program for houses of worship. The program's director, Stacey Kennealy, sums up the difference between the pre- and post-rubric work of GreenFaith as follows:

> In the past, we would often establish programs or set goals prematurely, without taking the time to reflect and assess. This approach, which served us well enough as a small New Jersey–based organization, wasn't workable as we outgrew our britches and became a strong national force. We needed a framework to set goals, evaluate progress over time, and assess "good," "better," "best."
>
> The "greening" rubric we created proved utterly transformative—after its completion it became apparent there was no program available to congregations to help them reach "Eden Restored." A need and niche for our work surfaced, which we fulfilled by launching the country's first interfaith environmental certification program. The program has been a clear win—there are over seventy-five congregations participating from half the states in the nation, participants are achieving success far beyond what we envisioned, and week after week there are front-page news stories about the program.

For me, an equally compelling story is what happened *internally* when GreenFaith started to think differently about assessment. Fletcher told me it had a galvanizing impact, with staff members becoming inspired to regularly revisit and strengthen the vision for GreenFaith's best work, and board members feeling more connected, more informed, and more engaged.

We should pause over the idea that GreenFaith's rubric on its program work had such an impact on the mind-set of the volunteers who govern the organization. It gave them a clearer, more detailed sense of what GreenFaith aspired to do and a far richer sense of what success would look like than the typical reports on how many institutions were being affected and how many people trained. And as a result of their engagement with the ideas of planning backward and ongoing improvement, before too long

> *The first value of the rubric was that it pushed us to think more clearly, and more deeply about what we were trying to accomplish. This turned out to be an exercise in vision development that was joyful for us. I don't mean to sound sappy, but it really was meaningful and fun.*
>
> *For the rubric to do its job, it needed to be a living part of our reality. We needed to talk about it, to tweak it, to critique it, to celebrate it. It needed to stay integrated as a part of the living mental landscape of our work.*
>
> *Over the years, we've found that the more we think about the rubrics we create, and the questions they evoke, the more we grow and develop in our ability to lead, in our effectiveness. Paying attention to the rubric is one of the best quality assurance practices I'm aware of. There's an implicit accountability involved in taking a rubric seriously, a self-judgment that has an edge to it. If you've spent time envisioning what success looks like to you, and you have felt an emotional and intellectual connection to that vision, you feel accountable to that vision. When you fall short, the shortcoming has an emotional price—it is disappointing to come up short.*
>
> Fletcher Harper, executive director, GreenFaith

Rubric 7.5: GreenFaith Board Assessment Rubric

Area of Board Life	Beginner, Burned Out, or in the Wrong Place	Growing Commitment
Board Membership's Life Impact - Personal - Time	Personal relationship with nature not deepened, consumption habits unchanged; advocacy not engaged.	Board member agrees that increased relationship with nature, greener consumption habits, advocacy are esteemed habits, but has not taken action. Board member enjoys meetings when present but resists time commitment. An hour per month or less given to GF.
Knowing and Communication - Knowledge of mission and priorities - Communication with peers	Board member cannot state mission and priorities, does not speak with friends, colleagues about GF's work.	Board member can articulate mission in several sentences or less, but cannot describe priorities. Board member mentions GF briefly in few conversations w/ peers.
Giving and Getting - Personal financial commitment - Cultivation of relationships	Giving/getting for GF is experienced as unpleasant. Personal financial commitment is minimal; no useful peers/personal contacts identified for cultivation.	Giving/getting is recognized as important; moderate level of personal giving in relation to means; delays in contacting peers/contacts for cultivation.
Committee Membership and Institutional Involvement	Board meeting attendance 50% or lower; no committee involvement.	Board meeting attendance 50 to 70%; inactive committee member.

the board decided to write a rubric for *themselves and their own performance*, as shown in rubric 7.5.

Fletcher reports that the board rubric allowed them to identify and value a number of components of board life, which gave all board members at least one or two areas in which they could shine. Having a place in the rubric (the indicators) to describe and celebrate effective performance kept momentum and excitement alive, and the rubric as a whole provided, in Fletcher's words, "a collectively affirmed ethos about how the board will function."

Standard Board Member	Outstanding Executive Committee Level
Personal relationship with nature strengthened, two or three consumption habits changed, periodic advocacy commitments made. Time commitments are anticipated and experienced as rewarding over 80% of the time. Board member gives two-plus hours a month to GF.	Personal relationship with nature deepened significantly, consumption habits greened and modeled for others, advocacy integrated into regular life. Board member enters into supportive relationships with other board members at earlier stages of board commitment; time commitment of four-plus hours per month.
Board member articulates mission in two sentences and concisely describe priorities; board member discusses GF proudly, regularly (three times a month) in conversations with friends.	Board member can accomplish all items in previous column and assist other board members in reaching that level of proficiency.
Giving/getting is engaged with curiosity and interest. GF is one of top two philanthropic priorities. One to two meetings organized annually with executive director and peers/contacts.	Giving/getting is deeply meaningful; GF is top philanthropic priority; board member connects executive director with helpful peers/contacts regularly; assists other board members in learning how to do this.
Board meeting attendance 75% plus; regular committee participation.	Board meeting attendance 90% plus; committee chair/leader; chair/leader of major initiative.

When I think of how many executive directors over the years have said they wished they had more engaged boards, I am moved by Fletcher's summary of how the board rubric has functioned: "The rubric establishes 'how we do things at GreenFaith.' This creates pride, a sense of identity, and strength. In addition, the presence of the rubric, and the fact that we treat our rubrics like evolving documents, has given board members the sense that they have a say, some control over the organization's developing vision for its board. It's very important."

— Evaluating a Core Practice: —
The Geraldine R. Dodge
Foundation Site Visit Rubric

At the same time I was urging our grantees to create rubrics to advance their own work, my program colleagues at the Geraldine R. Dodge Foundation and I took a stab at it ourselves. We asked ourselves the prompting question, *Is there a core performance to our work?* and we answered, *The site visit!* Even though we had many proposals to review each funding cycle, we took it as a matter of pride that we visited each organization personally, in order to better understand their work and to pay our respects.

We began brainstorming criteria for success and quickly realized we had three rubrics on our hands, or at least a rubric in three parts: "Quality of Preparation"; "Quality of Visit and Conversation"; and "Quality of Aftermath/Outcomes." For our levels of performance, we chose:

1	2	3	4
Poor	Okay	Our Standard:	Our Goal:
Unacceptable	Acceptable	Respect for Grantees	Exceeding the Standard

We wanted to have the next-to-top level be our standard, because a rubric should give you room to grow and improve. If you are already operating at the top of the rubric, it is not going to do you much good as a tool for improvement. We had recently done an exercise in which we identified our core values as a foundation, and "respect for grantees" was number one. Thus we used that phrase in the rubric, and it affected the way we filled the rubric out. Rubric 7.6 describes what happens—or should happen—before we even sit down with a social profit leader who has applied to the foundation for support.

Let's look at the descriptions of levels of performance regarding *logistics*. I like having a bottom to the rubric, because it allows you to describe poor or unacceptable behavior before it happens, thus minimizing the chances that it will. Plus in a healthy organization it gives you a space to describe the occasional screwup of an otherwise high-performing individual. As I noted in chapter 6, I am personally responsible for the phrase "shows up and they didn't know we were coming," having marked my calendar for a site visit with a theater company and then neglected to tell either my assistant or the theater company I had done so. On the other end of the spectrum, having defined Level 4, we made

Who's going to give the person in a position to recommend or decline a proposal honest feedback? Nobody. How long before you believe that no one minds it if you are late—or that you haven't read their proposal? Eager potential grantees would say, "You must be so busy." Or, "It's our fault you were late—our directions are hard to follow." The rubric washed all of that away. We created the exemplars and were able to self-monitor without feeling judged. I was able to hold myself accountable while simultaneously recognizing that the entire process is about continuous improvement and working toward mutually agreed upon standards. The result? Performance goes up and stress goes down. All that from a simple but elegant process that provided clarity around what excellence looks like.

Ross Danis, president and CEO,
Newark Trust for Education,
former program director,
Geraldine R. Dodge Foundation

Rubric 7.6: Dodge Foundation Site Visit Rubric Quality of Preparation

1 Poor, Unacceptable	2 Okay, Acceptable
Regarding substance: • Program officer skims proposal. • Doesn't know names of key people, or who's going to be at site visit. • Falls back on asking, "Would you walk me through this proposal?" • Says, "Can you come to our offices by noon tomorrow?"	Program officer reads proposal and report, has some questions prepared, knows who will be at the site visit.
Regarding logistics: Program officer has no idea how to find their office, leaves Dodge with no directions, map, or phone number. Program officer relies on instinct to find the right place and ends up in Moorestown instead of Morristown. Program officer requests last-minute meeting; or shows up and they didn't know we were coming; or is late and doesn't call; or gets confused and doesn't show up at all.	Program officer arranges for site visit over the phone when it makes sense for grantee and there is little to be gained from a face-to-face meeting (e.g., we know the grantee well or have just seen him/her).
Other considerations: Program officer schedules visits so tightly that he/she arrives too fried to do the site visit justice, or does not allow time to consolidate notes and understandings gained before moving on to something else.	

those additional phone calls when we could. Without the rubric, I am not sure we would have thought of it.

Rubric 7.7, the second of the three parts, looks at the site visit itself. We found that by creating a checklist of reminders for ourselves, we were also creating a valuable document to orient new program officers who joined our team.

DRAFT

3 Our Standard: Respect for Grantees	4 Our Goal: Exceeding the Standard
Program officer thoroughly reads proposal and report on last year's grant (in relation to specifics of grant letter); reviews last year's write-up to see what issues rose to the top; checks with colleagues in-house, and, when appropriate, in the field for any further background that sheds light on organizational health and/or work to be funded. Program officer develops questions that are not already answered in proposal.	Program officer expands own knowledge of field in appropriate way in preparation for visit and review. Program officer consults other supporting materials, becomes immersed in the big picture of grantee's work, aware of national trends and cycles of calendar year.
Grantees get sufficient notice, choice of time for meeting, advance notice of any major questions or concerns, and an opportunity to invite others they think important to the meeting. We ask if there is anything else they want us to see before the site visit. Grantee is clear about when we are showing up. Program officer leaves Dodge with all appropriate information, arrives at right place, at right time.	Program officer (or program assistant) makes phone call two or three days before the visit to confirm appointment and asks if there is any new information we should be aware of, or if there is anything on the grantee's mind that is not included in the proposal.
We have taken time to ask whether the right person is doing the site visit. We want to not fall off the fine line between social and professional; if program officer is a personal friend of grantee, we send someone else. We don't want one person to become the only contact and champion for an organization.	We view the relationship with grantee within a yearlong cycle. More than one of us is in contact during the year; we have conversations that are not about the proposal under review. We remember that funders don't have all the answers and behave accordingly. We are partners with our grantees to improve society.

The site visit rubric once again demonstrates the wisdom of having the next-to-highest level of the rubric be impressive in its own right. If we performed at the level of "Our Standard: Respect for Grantees," we were doing a good job. But the rubric asked us to describe what an even higher level might look like. It's a great question for the program team at any foundation to ponder.

Rubric 7.7: Dodge Foundation Site Visit Rubric
Quality of Visit and Conversation

1 Poor, Unacceptable	2 Okay, Acceptable
Program officer: • Conveys aura of mystery about what we do and how we do it. • Asks questions they have already answered in the proposal. • Lets frustrations come out when things are not going well with the organization. • Takes no notes and leaves the visit with no specific information. • Takes a cell phone call in the middle of the visit. • Loses sight of grantor/grantee relationship.	Program officer: • Goes to them, at their convenience, on time, with appropriate attire. • Has informed conversation about the proposal and lets them know when they will hear from us. • Asks if they have any questions for us.

Remember that rubrics work both ways: they can shape behavior and they can also capture it for others to learn from. In chapter 5, when one of the servers greeted Mr. Yingling by name, the rubric changed for the better. The same thing happened on the third page of our site visit rubric (rubric 7.8). One of my colleagues came up with a great way to live the value of "Respect for Grantees." He decided to have pre-addressed and stamped postcards with him when he made a site visit so that the first thing he would do when he got back to his car was write a quick note of thanks, with some detail of the conversation he had particularly appreciated. Time for him: maybe a minute. Effect on grantee: priceless. We made it part of our Level 4 for "Quality of Aftermath/Outcomes."

DRAFT

3 Our Standard: Respect for Grantees	4 Our Goal: Exceeding the Standard
Program officer: • Places the visit in a context: The past relationship is known and valued. • Asks the right questions of the right people; knows who does what and who thinks about what. • Is aware of life-cycle issues, does not have the same conversation year after year. • Is clear about the process: when things happen, how many groups are being considered, when and how grantee can still communicate with us, etc. • Recognizes the value of grantee's time. • Expresses appreciation for grantee's work, regardless of outcome of specific grant proposal. • Takes notes sufficient enough to inform the write-up, but not so much as to not be fully present in the conversation. *(Wait a minute. That's great. I need to write that down.)* • Clearly maintains the balance between the social and the professional. • Gives even more time to groups likely to be declined, so they know they have been heard.	Program officer: • Intervenes and significantly changes the conversation for the better by getting to important things that need to be said. • Acts as a resource, or consultant; connects group to others in a helpful way; helps brainstorm about the future in a productive way. • Notes impressions and body language, asks *What are they trying to convey to me?*

I'll state the obvious. We were conducting a very personal style of philanthropy. It is the kind you can do if you are rooted in place—in our case, New Jersey—and you have many long-standing relationships with grantees. Our rubric would not have been appropriate for a large national foundation, or for a small family foundation without the staff to carry it off. The point is that it was ours. It made us better in ways that we had decided mattered to us. It brought us closer together as colleagues because it underscored our sense of identity and shared values. And I know our grantees, as well as those we visited but did not fund, appreciated much-deserved respect.

Rubric 7.8: Dodge Foundation Site Visit Rubric
Aftermath Outcomes

1 Poor, Unacceptable	2 Okay, Acceptable
Program officer: • Forgets about the visit. • Forgets to send information or names as promised during the site visit. • Moves on to something else with nothing to show for having made the visit.	Program officer: • Makes notes sufficient enough to provide details for case for funding. • Follows through on any clear promises.

This assessment model adapted for philanthropy is provocative and limitless in positioning the field to live up to its promise of being a social change "passing lane." I think the missing piece is including and working with grantees to co-create a site visit rubric that puts the grantee voice in a more central position. What if in meeting with a grantee for the first time, or in refreshing a relationship with a long-term grantee, we began with a site visit rubric exercise together? I have a feeling that we could model participatory democracy and a new civic engagement model around grant-making and grantee–funder relationships. I hope there will be an online Community of Practice that enables rubrics to become dynamic tools to enhance professional development and best practice in the field.

Michelle Knapik, president and CEO,
Tremaine Foundation

DRAFT

3 Our Standard: Respect for Grantees	4 Our Goal: Exceeding the Standard
Program officer: • Organizes impressions and understandings quickly, through dictation into recorder or list of bullet points. • Notes any to-do items, such as promising to send a book or a reference, or promising to get grantee in touch with someone; follows through quickly on these items. • Keeps colleagues at Dodge informed about what's been learned, particularly regarding points that may affect other reviews. • Checks in with any partner organizations in work to be funded.	Program officer: • Sends an email or card after the visit thanking them for their time. • Makes effort to see the program we have learned about taking place; makes follow-up visit to observe firsthand what was talked about during the site visit. • Follows up not only on promised connections but also thinks, *Who else should this grantee know about?*; makes connections, even cross-sector. • Calls others in the field who are connected to or affected by grantee's work, so as to incorporate those views and perspectives into the write-up for the board.

8

Rubrics for Sustainability

You bump into the word *sustainability* almost as often as *measurement* in the civic sector these days—an interesting juxtaposition since sustainability is among the hardest of social aspirations to measure. Many dislike the word because it seems too vague, too all-encompassing. But that is why I like it. It invites a vision of the future that is long-range, inclusive, and highly functional, and as a form of social profit it will appropriately vary from place to place. I have come to think the proper response to someone invoking the concept of sustainability is not an exasperated "What does *that* mean?" but rather an interested "What do *you* mean? And who else is in on it?"[17]

Rubrics lend themselves particularly well to the task of describing complicated, multipart visions such as sustainability. In this chapter I will present two organizations that have begun to use rubrics in this way—the Emerald Cities Collaborative (ECC) and the Institute for Sustainable Communities (ISC).

— Emerald Cities Collaborative —

Emerald Cities Collaborative (ECC) is a national network of organizations working together to advance a sustainable environment while creating economic opportunities for all. Their distinctive niche has been in bringing together various interests in a city—business, labor, government, community organizations—to promote an equitable approach to new jobs in the green energy economy.

There are ten Emerald Cities in the United States, and work is under way in eight of them to build collaborative approaches to large-scale retrofits and community and workforce development, while championing the concept of a triple bottom line (equity, environment, economy) in their cities. But the cities, ranging from Providence, Rhode Island, to Portland, Oregon, from Milwaukee to San Francisco, are not all starting in the same place, and they have different opportunities based on who sits at the table of their local councils. Thus a team of ECC local directors devised a rubric for describing success that takes into account local differences.

Their "High Road Rubric" reflects their long-range ideal vision of an Emerald City while allowing flexibility for each city to define its own short- and medium-term goals on the way to achieving that high level of success. The rubric identifies a menu of important quantitative measures in each area of the triple bottom line, and urges the local directors and councils to choose from among them for the ones most appropriate to measure in their city. Finally, most important, the rubric format allows for *qualitative* description as well. The basic format, the starting place for all the Emerald Cities, is presented in rubric 8.1.

Some cities had a sustainability "baseline" that has allowed ECC to build on existing momentum. Before becoming an Emerald City, Portland, Oregon, for example, already had a City Green Building Policy, a County Climate Action Plan, and a State Renewable Energy Portfolio Standard, project labor agreements, and workforce training systems in place. The city also had conducted a disparity study and implemented aspirational public policies for diversity in hiring. The Bay Area cities of San Francisco and Oakland have California's Global Warming Solutions Act, which commits the state to reducing greenhouse gas emissions to 1990 levels by 2020, and Seattle has its Climate Action Plan to help it reach its goal of being carbon-neutral by 2050. The annual goals and activities and three- to five-year goals vary according to these starting places and other local conditions, but the touchstone for all Emerald Cities is articulated in the far-right column, the Emerald Green Vision, which is the aspirational "top of the rubric."

We see the rubric as an important and helpful organizational tool. ECC is challenged by its three-fold mission (environment, economy, equity), and its nationwide, multi-site geography. The rubric helps to organize our work and our coalitions within and across our local sites. While we are still in the early stages of using the rubric, the yearlong process of developing it provided the basis for coherent, albeit difficult, conversations among different sets of actors across different sites and about different objectives, as well as for building consensus about what success looks like. Going forward, I expect the rubric will help us know what we are doing and how well we are doing it. I can envision some great strategy sessions with our local councils on a range of common issues. In sum, the rubric gives us greater capacity, locally and nationally, to find the right points of leverage for the transformation we seek, and it will enhance our ability to muster the right tools and resources to achieve it.

Denise Fairchild, president and CEO,
Emerald Cities Collaborative

Rubric 8.1: The ECC Triple Bottom Line Rubric Template

City:	Date:

Local Mission Statement:		
Categories to Measure Goals and Key Measures	**Baseline: Status at Point of ECC Engagement**	**Current Status: includes Previous Year Achievements**
Time Frame	Month/Year: 7/13	Year Ending: 12/14
Environmental Goals		
Number of sustainability agreements with description		
Public policy that drives demand for Energy Efficiency (EE)		
Other efforts to drives		
Number of ECC building audits Number of ECC building retrofits Sectors with active EE programs		
Energy savings (kBtu/yr)/avg % Water savings (kGal/yr)/avg% Renewable energy (kBtu/yr) avg %		
GHG reduction (metric tons)		
Economic Goals		
Number of agreements with commitments to job creation		
Policies recognizing EE as economic driver and requiring local job creation and business participation		
Number of high-road jobs (FTEs)		
Number of workers Number of apprentices		
Payroll $ for construction jobs		
$ invested in ECC projects		
Revenue generated for local business (city headquarters)		

Local Director:	Local Council Review:

Annual Goals and Activities	3- to 5-Year Goals	Emerald Green Vision
Year: 2015	Target Year: 2020	
		Organizational and municipal sustainability plans have carbon reduction targets aligned with global standards.
		Public policy has enforcement authority for carbon reduction.
		Zero net energy buildings (New Buildings Institute).
		ECC drives all MUSH+ and affordable housing sector projects.
		All buildings are Energy Star certified, or equivalent.
		Majority of ECC projects use renewable or alternative energy. 10% of buildings are Net Zero projects.
		Market transformation achieved; there is economic and equity inclusion in the energy efficiency sector and the sector is seen as a long-term driver for the economy.
		All jobs in energy sector are high-road jobs, with integrated education and training infrastructure.
		Economic development in other sectors includes triple bottom line principles.
		All investments in building retrofits use local contractors and a local workforce, strengthening the local economy.

Rubric 8.1: The ECC Triple Bottom Line Rubric Template (continued)

Categories to Measure Goals and Key Measures	Baseline: Status at Point of ECC Engagement	Current Status: Includes Previous Year Achievements
Equity Goals		
Number of agreements with commitment to equity		
Diversity of stakeholder groups and participation level in ECC coalition		
Strength of coalition and commitment of partners		
Policy, legislation, and regulations ensuring equity and efforts toward their passage		
Number of events and hearings to drive the triple bottom line		
Employment access: % minority % women % local hires % retention of targeted groups (after one year). Include specific populations (i.e., African American) where possible.		
% of disadvantaged businesses (including number of primes, tier 1, tier 2, etc.)		
Resources and training programs Workers Disadvantaged businesses		
Number and % of disadvantaged apprentices (specific populations where possible)		
Number and % pre-apprenticeship graduates		
% retention of targeted apprentices		

Annual Goals and Activities	3- to 5-Year Goals	Emerald Green Vision
		City-wide ECC coalition of interests: active alliances among labor, business, and community organizations.
		High-road principles are widely understood and required within the larger community and included in all public contracts and programs.
		Disadvantaged communities have access to career opportunities, and workplace reflects local demographics.
		Systematic inclusion of underrepresented communities in workforce, training, and development.
		Established and effective systems that train and support a diverse workforce.
		Regional and continuous support for building the capacity of disadvantaged businesses.
		All projects use a minimum of 15% apprentices, one third from disadvantaged communities or targeted pre-apprenticeship programs.

In its early use, the rubric has become a tool for communication and ongoing learning at ECC as well as for describing and reckoning success. President and CEO Denise Fairchild writes, "Looking at our local councils' recently-completed rubrics has not only given me a bird's-eye view of what we need to do at the national level to scale up our impact, it also has allowed me to understand how the national staff can be more helpful and strategic in ensuring success at the local level." It has also broadened her sense of leverage points. "While we have focused on retrofitting large public, institutional, and multifamily buildings to be energy and water efficient," she says, "I now recognize the strategic importance of our local councils undertaking policy work such as utility reform and carbon reduction legislation."

The key for ECC will be finding the right pace for the rubric work—indeed, for the collaborative's work as a whole—because the cast of characters is large, varied, and changing, and they operate in a charged political environment. At its best, if people become comfortable using it, the rubric will help them know where they are and where they are heading at a glance, in relation to the goals and objectives they have identified together as being at the heart of their vision.

— Institute for Sustainable Communities —

The Institute for Sustainable Communities (ISC), based in Montpelier, Vermont, believes in citizen-driven change around the world. ISC began its work supporting fledgling democracies in Eastern Europe in establishing civil societies and addressing pressing environmental, social, and economic challenges. Over time, the ISC staff and board have expanded their areas of expertise and their organizational impact, with emphasis on the challenges of urbanization and climate disruption. Their work now ranges from training factory managers in Asia about the principles and practices of sustainable manufacturing to providing technical assistance to some two hundred US communities developing sustainability plans.

While Emerald Cities decided to combine their goals into a single rubric, the Institute for Sustainable Communities took a different approach. Fresh off a strategic plan, they choose to write a rubric defining what success would look like for each of the specific objectives in their plan. The resulting rubrics range from specific program objectives on urban sustainability and sustainable manufacturing to ongoing organizational goals regarding

1	2	3	4
Unacceptable Level	Minimally Acceptable	High, Perfectly Acceptable Level	Exemplary Level

communications and staff learning. For each objective, the staff describes performance and outcomes on four levels:

Typically we gravitate to the top of rubrics like this; after all, that is where we describe what we are really looking to achieve. But ISC vice president for institutional advancement Barbara McAndrew explains the value of having the whole spectrum: "Working through the rubrics as a team made a difference to us. The conversation itself becomes part of who we are and infiltrates planning and implementation. And, while it is great to articulate the inspirational, I also appreciate the requirement to identify the unacceptable—the line over which we will not cross. It's practical. You don't have to belabor it or stay in a negative space but it really helps align everyone."

You can appreciate how important her last point is to an organization that currently has offices, staff, and programs in five different countries: the United States, China, Bangladesh, India, and Serbia. President and CEO George Hamilton sums up his sense of how rubrics benefit ISC: "The real challenge for sustainability is how to measure across multiple disciplines and sectors. If you are an environmental group, you can measure air quality. If you are a social justice group, you can measure jobs. But if you are trying to create holistic thinking, that is a more complex measure, and that's why qualitative measures are even more important. The greatest part about developing rubrics is that it gets people on the same page as far as what success is, and they know where they fit. This is at the heart of alignment."

Rubric 8.2: ISC Rubric on Training and Continuous Improvement at EHS Centers

Objective: Define and establish a quality control system that ensures excellent training and continuous improvement in all EHS+ Centers, and by 2016, train at least 8,000 managers annually through the EHS+ Network

	1 Unacceptable Level	2 Minimally Acceptable
Curriculum	1. None/poor quality 2. Basic topics only or incomplete 3. Irrelevant 4. Outdated 5. Culturally insensitive; "ist" 6. No training objectives	1. Basic, intermediate, advanced core set defined 2. Annual review 3. Up-to-date content 4. EHS+ (2013 curriculum as minimum) 5. Courses classified by industry 6. Theory of business case in all courses 7. Courses delivered in interesting way (client not bored)
Training	1. Training the wrong people 2. Not consistent across centers 3. Insufficient training management system 4. Poor trainers 5. No training/trainer assessment and qualification system 6. No logistical support/poor logistics 7. Poor communication with clients	1. Courses delivered consistently, in timely way 2. Meet standard for course delivery 3. Positive client feedback 4. Clients not surprised 5. Client learns something 6. Low dropout rate 7. Trainer utilization < 30%

Let's look at just one of ISC's rubrics and how it is being used. The second major goal in the ISC strategic plan is "To advance EHS (Environment, Health, and Safety) compliance and sustainable manufacturing practices in Asia." They are building on the success of existing EHS centers in China, and indeed their first objective is to establish a network of these centers in China, India, and Bangladesh. A second objective has to do with quality control and impact of these centers, as described in rubric 8.2.

3 High, Perfectly Acceptable Level	4 Exemplary Level
1. Courses updated rapidly as needed 2. Curriculum content accountability clearly defined 3. Annual survey of customer needs 4. Curriculum Review Committee 5. Demonstrating "business case" in most courses 6. Centralized system for managing curriculum resources (network) used	1. Recognized externally as state-of-the-art content/ curriculum innovator 2. Proactively develop curriculum 3. Majority of courses have industry-adapted version 4. EHS+ centers generate new data on "business case"
1. Trainers are inspiring 2. Create loyal clients, clients recommending course to others 3. Zero complaints 4. Trainee comes back to be guest speaker	1. Transformation (client) 2. Factory behavior improved 3. Gurus (trainers) 4. Community of alumni donors

Rubric 8.2 (continued)

	1 Unacceptable Level	2 Minimally Acceptable
Leadership (communication, leadership, advocacy)	1. Not part of course	1. Basic concepts in stand-alone course 2. Training of trainers
Measurement & learning evaluation	1. No commitment to quality management/ outcome tracking 2. No staff to implement 3. System not in place 4. No data tracking system in place 5. Participant data not collected 6. Inconsistent tools for collecting data 7. Outcome expectations not aligned with ISC's 8. No theory of change	1. M&E role among team 2. Indicator tracking 3. Basic data analysis done (dashboard) 4. Data meets donor requirements 5. Data tracking system in place (Excel) 6. Participant data collection system in place 7. Share data with ISC 8. Theory of change documented/reviewed 9. At least one data collection method used 10. Customer feedback captured and addressed 11. Data analysis at least annual 12. Trainees receive basic briefing on data expectations 3 months (advocacy) 6 months (factory level)
EHS managers	1. "Came and forgot" 2. No change in behavior	
Certification	1. Not having one 2. Having one, but not offering it	1. Basic certification standards defined 2. Industry assessment completed
Factory owners	Not engaged	
Quality control system		

3 High, Perfectly Acceptable Level	4 Exemplary Level
1. Advanced topics in stand-alone and integrated across all courses 2. Improved communication & advocacy skills	1. Change agents
1. Dedicated M&E staff 2. Indicator tracking 3. Center integrates data into planning and program improvement 4. Center adapts theory of change based on data 5. Seamless integration of data in client management 6. 12 month (factory)	1. Thought leaders 2. Break new ground on data collection and application 3. Evidence-based institution 4. Learning organization 5. White papers by centers
1. Rigorous system in place and enforced 2. New standard for the profession defined/what constitutes excellence 3. Career path created 4. X% of level specific 5. Z% technical specific 6. Y% full certification	1. Government accreditation 2. Market standard for certification 3. EHS+ (leadership) (establishing a new profession)

This is the first draft of this rubric, and I am grateful to ISC for allowing me to use it here in its unfinished form. As important as what is in the rubric is how it got there, for the process reveals the power of the rubric to bring people together. ISC vice president for international programs Michael Despines and program director for Asia Matthew DeGroot met with staff from China, India, and Bangladesh for a day and a half and produced "a document we can use as our road map and compass," according to Despines. The process, he says, "allowed us to establish a shared vision for the project and a common understanding of what we were trying

> *The rubric will provide a valuable reference point on our progress with the project. We will refer to it quarterly as a way to allow us to remind ourselves of what we said was important and verify if we are on track. Are we making the right investments? Are we spending enough time and effort on the most important project elements? And we may find that we need to update or modify the rubric based on our experience and learning in the field. That is fine also. The rubric provides a structured touchstone to allow us to have these important conversations and assess if we are on track. My staff have repeatedly and enthusiastically told me that the process was very useful and valuable. Many have commented though that if we really want to ensure that the rubric is relevant, then we should incorporate elements of it into each staff person's performance management planning to ensure accountability.*
>
> Michael Despines, vice president
> for international programs,
> Institute for Sustainable Communities

to achieve. Often, each person has a different understanding or interpretation of project intentions, elements, or priorities." So the rubric became a tool for eliminating that lack of clarity.

The ISC program leaders followed up via Survey Monkey with copies of the draft rubric to various stakeholders, asking "Is this right? What are we missing?" Used in this way, the rubric becomes a vehicle for ongoing education, inclusion, and refinement of both vision and action plans. As DeGroot says, "The more you do this the better you get. It is liberating; we are creating an internal dialogue and a process for checking in."

The ISC draft rubric raises an interesting question that should be considered with any rubric: When, if ever, does it stop being a draft and become a touchstone? Put another way, should you put the rubric on the wall and come back to it every six months or so to use it to see what sort of progress you are making, or should you continuously revise and improve the rubric based on what you are learning? I do not think there is a hard-and-fast answer to this question, but my inclination, as I said in chapter 6, is to take any rubric out for a test drive before putting it on any wall. Rubrics are always improved by experience, and they evolve with changing circumstances and opportunities. The key is to remember that it is not the rubric itself that matters; it is the social profit the rubric allows us to define and pursue accordingly.

9

Rubrics for Larger Systems

THE RUBRIC EXAMPLES IN CHAPTER 7 came from organizations with single offices, where the staffs can sit around a table together. In chapter 8, we looked at two organizations with multiple offices, operating in different geographic locations. Now let's look at how rubrics can help create larger systems through which multiple organizations can cooperate and coordinate efforts.

—— A Foundational Rubric: —— Whole Measures

The story of Whole Measures begins with the national environmental organization I mentioned in chapter 3, the Trust for Public Land (TPL). The rubric that stemmed from the TPL retreat in Wisconsin has evolved into a promising tool for defining social profit in areas as diverse as food systems and storm relief. Let's begin with a section of the TPL rubric itself, which you may remember was designed to allow TPL staff across the country to describe success in conservation projects beyond acres and dollars. Rubric 9.1 shows a sample page.

Rubric 9.1: TPL Mission Rubric on Justice and Fairness

(Negative) −1	(Neutral) 0	(Modest) 1
The result is exclusive and private use of the land. TPL's work interferes with the use of the land by a non-dominant culture. The projects' primary benefits are to people who are wealthy or already have higher-than-average benefits from parks and recreation lands.	TPL's work doesn't explicitly protect use of the land by a non-dominant culture, but it benefits people across the demographic spectrum fairly proportionately.	The park or conservation land is particularly valued by or accessible to people of below-average income or groups that are underserved by traditional park and open space systems. TPL is working in partnership with groups dedicated to environmental, social, and racial justice.

The use of numbers across the top of the rubric is illuminating. At the bottom of the rubric is not a 1 but a −1. The folks at TPL—whose catchphrase is *Conserving land for people*—had undoubtedly experienced pangs of regret when a conservation deal had resulted in "exclusive and private use of the land," but now they are saying it will literally *subtract* from their reckoning of success if this or any of their other criteria are neglected.

People who like precise measures may raise an eyebrow over a phrase like "fundamental human respect for nature." Yet TPL's purpose at the top of their rubric is not precise measurement but rather the beginning of a conversation about their highest aspirations: what success would *really* look like. Imagine staffers discussing how to turn a Level 2 project into a Level 3; all projects will benefit. Imagine the rubric expanding with stories of the one or two projects a year that reach the top level of the rubric; more accomplishments at this level will almost certainly follow.

Another of the criteria they identify in the twelve-part rubric is "civic engagement." At the −1 level, there is disenfranchisement, polarization, and/or alienation, and just above that there is no

(Strong) 2	(Exemplary) 3
TPL's work is making significant progress in correcting inequities, e.g., helping an Indian tribe regain the use of lands that are important for cultural or economic purposes; adding parks in low-income neighborhoods that fall below minimum standards for access to parks. TPL's work creates change within the community by building support, fostering institutions, or generating resources that have widespread beneficial impacts on justice and fairness.	The park or conservation effort redresses a widely perceived injustice and is widely recognized for its significance. TPL's work leads to a meaningful and lasting change in policy by governments, foundations, or NGOs to promote justice and fairness in access to parks and conservation lands. Our work illustrates the fundamental human respect for nature. This project elevates what it means to be human by addressing our human sense of fairness toward all life.

outreach or local involvement at all. It is the top two levels that, as always, inspire planning backward. TPL staff members all over the country were involved in the creation of this rubric and as a result had a new, shared frame of reference as they approached their work from Georgia to Alaska. For "Strong," the next-to-highest level, they wrote:

> *The project helps a community become more self-aware. The standard of citizenship is raised as more people rally around a common conservation cause, and thus the public sphere is expanded, and opposing forces are brought together in healthy debate about a wide range of issues.*
>
> *The conservation effort avoids a change in land use that would have broken important community bonds. Benefits of this land extend beyond a local community to a regional constituency.*

I am sure you are used to the pattern by now: This level sounds like something worthy to aspire to. But then there is the top of the rubric, an even more ambitious vision of success. For an "Exemplary" level of civic engagement, they wrote:

> *TPL's work galvanizes the community to better understand itself, work together, shift political structures, and create significant new social capital.*
>
> *Working with TPL, many different sectors of the community develop a sustained commitment to conservation efforts.*
>
> *The community recognizes the connection between parks or land conservation and other fundamental issues of life such as education, justice, and common welfare.*
>
> *Benefits of this land extend to a national constituency.*

The scale and ambition of the TPL rubric have inspired others to adapt it for different uses. The Center for Whole Communities in Vermont expanded its scope, creating the remarkable Whole Measures framework for planning, implementing, and measuring change. As its name implies, the Whole Measures framework encourages communities to embrace a wide variety of values, including those that are hard to quantify. As cities and towns plan for their futures, Whole Measures helps them think about social equity as well as jobs, ecosystem health along with economic vitality.

— Adapting the Whole Measures — Rubric to Food System Work

Recently, the Whole Measures framework has been applied very powerfully to the worlds of food security and community food systems. The composition of the working group that developed Whole Measures for Community Food Systems (CFS) over fifteen months is worth pausing over, because it reveals the cultural and geographic diversity of this effort: Jeanette Abi-Nader, Community Food Security Coalition (Oregon); Adrian Ayson, Center for Whole Communities (Vermont); Keecha Harris, Keecha Harris and Associates, Inc. (Alabama); Hank Herrera, Center for Popular Research, Education, and Policy (California); Darcel Eddins, Bountiful Cities Project (North Carolina); Deb Habib, Seeds of Solidarity (Massachusetts); Jim Hanna; Chris Paterson, Center for Popular Research, Education, and Policy (Vermont); Karl Sutton, Sustainable Lives (Washington); Lydia Villanueva, CASA del Llano (Texas).

Whole Measures CFS includes six fields of practice within the world of community food system development: Justice and Fairness; Strong Communities; Vibrant Farms; Healthy People; Sustainable Ecosystems; and Thriving Local Economies. Not surprisingly, success in this framework is values-based, and it is integrated. These values need one another, and Whole Measures CFS is designed to help everyone see the whole system. At the same time, Whole Measures CFS looks closely at each of these fields, and suggests four specific practices in each area that bring their holistic vision to life; for each of the practices it suggests two to four possible outcomes. Groups that will be using the framework are encouraged to consider all of these practices and outcomes and adapt them so that they will be measuring what matters to them.

Let me give some examples to help you see how it works. Under "Justice and Fairness," the document presents these four practices:

1. Provides food for all.
2. Reveals, challenges, and dismantles injustice in the food system.

3. Creates just food system structures and cares for food
   system workers.
4. Ensures that public institutions and local businesses
   support a just community food system.

Every one of these practices is then followed by possible outcomes.
Here are the outcomes presented for the fourth practice, which
involves public institutions and businesses:

- Ensures that schools and other public institutions serve
  healthy and delicious meals to all and gives preference to
  purchasing food from local farms.
- Sustains stores in every community that sell healthy, high-
  quality, affordable foods.
- Supports local food processing and distribution efforts that
  are viable and that create safe, healthy, and meaningful liveli-
  hoods for all those who work in the food system.

Under "Healthy People," the document presents these four
practices:

1. Provides healthy food for all.
2. Ensures the health and well-being of all people, inclusive of
   race and class.
3. Connects people and the food system, from field to fork.
4. Connects people and land to promote health and wellness.

And under the third of those practices, connecting people and the
food system, we see these possible outcomes:

- Promotes a range of diverse connections between local food
  producers and consumers.
- Increases knowledge of the connections between food
  quality, healthy environments, and healthy people.

- Commits resources to teach people of all ages the skills and knowledge essential to food production, preparation, nutrition, and enjoyment.

In short, the approach is comprehensive, and the numerous outcomes are specific enough to be actionable. With each area, practice, and outcome, the Whole Measures CFS uses the rubric format to encourage people, organizations, and coalitions to measure their progress and success along a five-point scale, from "Negative Impact" to "Neutral" to "Some Impact" to "Strong Impact" to "Highest Impact." The numerical values assigned to these levels have grown since the original TPL rubric; "Negative Impact" is a –3, and "Highest Impact is a +10.

The forty-page *Whole Measure CFS* booklet is available on several websites.[18] It is the fullest application of formative assessment principles in the social sector that I have yet seen. It carefully defines its terms and offers extensive discussion guides at the end. As the authors say, they are interested not only in *doing things right*, but also in *doing the right things*, and they know that the best results will come when everyone in the field is pursuing those ends and learning from one another. Their comprehensive rubric holds and advances the conversation.

Doing work collaboratively and comprehensively is not for the impatient or fainthearted. Jeanette Abi-Nader, one of the original adaptors of Whole Measures to CFS, tells me, "We spent a year and a half collaboratively developing the Community Food Systems version with input from hundreds of grantees and practitioners. Then we hosted train-the-trainer type workshops for two years to build capacity to implement the tool. Then we spent another year and a half on a mentoring project with about a dozen organizations, aimed at understanding how *Whole Measure CFS* was being used."

She says the tool was used primarily at first as a frame for strategic planning and thinking and a way for organizations (and individuals) to understand how their work fits into a broader whole.

With those frameworks and understandings in place, the tool has begun to be used for evaluation. The process has also produced a companion publication, *Stories from the Field*, which shares how nine groups are using the *Whole Measure CFS* tool in their communities. Finally, in her comment below, Jeanette underscores the importance of rubric design coming from the inside out rather than the outside in.

One final thought is about the language associated with the tool. The Whole Measures frame may be helpful to push a dominant culture group to consider concepts like justice and fairness and storytelling, But for a non-dominant culture group that already communicates through storytelling—and faces institutionalized racism daily—the idea of sitting down with a rubric to capture what you are already doing as core to your work is an academic practice at best and a potential waste of precious time and resources. We worked to develop the community food systems version with language from groups on the ground doing the work. And still, some groups had to "translate" and modify the language to make it meaningful to youth or to neighborhood groups or to community activists.

This difficulty in utilizing whole measures (not just the tool but the concept) is not really a difficulty but a characteristic of the change process and of aiming to think holistically. It is fully energizing to be developing systems that work to tell the whole story of our change efforts.

Jeanette Abi-Nadir, organizational development, evaluation, and community food justice consulting

— The Sandy Connection: Adapting the — Whole Measures Approach to Storm Relief

In the aftermath of Hurricane Sandy's devastating impact on the Jersey shore, two statewide funders, the Dodge Foundation and the Community Foundation of New Jersey, wanted to frame the recovery efforts as the beginning of a long-term collaborative effort among funders and grantees that established and advanced an agenda of resiliency, plus accountability for policy makers and state and local governments. Their goals were to highlight the contributions and innovative approaches of the social profit sector, leverage the impact of grants through networks and collaborations, and raise the level of conversation around issues of equity.

These funders knew a good assessment strategy with public benchmarks would be essential for educating the public as well as for advancing best practices in resilient community development and disaster relief work. So they turned to Ginny McGinn, executive director of the Center for Whole Communities, for help with applying the Whole Measures approach to the New Jersey Recovery Fund (NJRF). Twenty-three organizations, representing the Arts, Planning and Environment, and Media, participated in drafting the rubric. The work is unfolding as I write.

The product of this collaboration so far is six worksheets, each organized around a rubric on one of the elements of their vision of success. The six elements are: Community Connectivity and Engagement; Economic Vitality (ensuring the long-term economic vitality of coastal and inland communities); Healthy Ecosystems & Healthy Habitat for People; Justice & Fairness (fostering equity); Public Information and Telling the Story; and Collaboration (creating collective impact). Each worksheet has from four to nine specific objectives, and success in relation to those objectives is described along the same spectrum used by the

Community Food Systems group: from Negative (–3) to Highest Impact (+10).

It is not my purpose here to convey the comprehensive nature of the NJRF rubric. But I would like to use it as a further example of how the rubric format helped a group to identify what mattered most to them—in this case, what elements would be critical to long-term success in anticipating, dealing with, and recovering from the future storms that most climate scientists predict.

The difference between the top and bottom of the rubric defines a huge spectrum; its creators are in effect describing two different worlds. For example, on the first worksheet on community engagement, Objective 1.03 is: "Build awareness and understanding of sea level rise, climate change, and potential impacts on New Jersey," and the ends of the rubric are anchored as follows:

At a Negative (–3) level: Inaccurate information is disseminated about the impacts of sea level rise and climate change and the potential impacts on New Jersey's future.

At a Highest Impact (+10) level: There is a state- and community-wide acceptance that New Jersey must develop a new state approach to preparing for a more resilient future by intervening in a rapidly changing system, to ensure the vitality of natural resources as well as the built environment. There is strong public support for all strategies.

And, as you have seen before, the difference between the next-to-highest and highest levels of the rubric is designed to set a high bar for success. On the worksheet on economic vitality, Objective 2.03 is "Quantify and communicate the costs as well as benefits of the current tourism industry." As we have come to expect, the next-to-highest level is impressive, even ambitious:

At the Strong (+5) level: Across the state there is an accurate understanding of both costs and benefits of the tourism industry and the benefits that natural capital provides. Decisions impacting the industry are made considering a more accurate analysis of natural capital, balancing community interests and needs with business interests.

But the rubric also illustrates what success would *really* look like:

At the Highest Impact (+10) level: Leaders across nonprofit, government, and business sectors are actively sharing information and strategies to optimize tourism's contribution to the New Jersey economy while protecting natural and community resources in the process. Industry growth and development exemplify these strategies.

The top of the rubric poses questions that might not otherwise be asked: Are we set up to share information? What strategies are we talking about? What do natural and community resources need protecting from? Where else in the country has industry growth and development "exemplified" the strategic balance being described, and what can we learn from their experience?

I like that the foundation members in the group are specifically identifying that long-term collaboration will require different behavior from them. On the sixth worksheet, Objective 6.06 is: "Increase and pool philanthropic resources to advance common goals associated with a resilient recovery." Look at the contrast between their descriptions of future success at the ends of the rubric:

At the Negative (−3) level: Philanthropy returns to regular grant-making strategies, working competitively with little or no communication among grant makers, causing the big-picture, collaborative work to drop and nonprofits to return to specific work for specific funds. Communities are left to pick up the pieces on their own.

At the Highest Impact (+10) level: Funders come together eighteen months after the storm (and on a regular basis thereafter) to assess recovery progress and recommit funds to long-term resiliency solutions. Philanthropic boards understand investments now will reduce future emergency investments and collectively agree to increase payout for five to seven years to respond to long-term resiliency efforts.

Much of the value of the rubric lies in the collaborative and individual processes that grantee organizations underwent in participating in it. Utilizing the rubric gave grantee organizations an opportunity to step back and take a wider-angle view on their programmatic activity and to reflect on the strategy of an integrated recovery process. The rubric was designed to encourage a holistic view and to bring diverse indicators and objectives to the forefront for organizations that may not have otherwise considered the various pieces of the recovery puzzle. Filling out the rubric gave grantees an opportunity for strategic analysis and reflection in the six issue areas, as well as an opportunity to network and share ideas across issue focus areas. It encouraged participants to think of their impacts outside of their usual siloed areas of direct impact, and perhaps seeded ideas of how to strengthen impact. We hope that the engagement in this process can be supportive to successful cross-sectoral collaboration.

From the Whole Measures Assessment Report
for the New Jersey Recovery Fund

If the foundations are not able to perform at that self-described highest level, it will not be because the vision was never articulated.

The NJRF team will present the work to progressively wider groups of grantees and eventually the public, using the practice of writing DRAFT across the top, as they foster the collaborations and partnerships that are part of their long-term vision. As with all rubrics, there will be room to add specific program indicators along the way to help people understand what specifically constitutes or represents different levels of success. The challenge of work like this, of course, is keeping the attention of busy people when their memories of a storm like Sandy start to fade. Will the work start to feel theoretical rather than necessary? Will foundations continue to fund work that does not have current results they can point to directly? All we can say is that even if the NJRF itself goes dormant, the process will have had an effect on mind-sets, relationships, and behaviors that will benefit New Jersey when the next big storm hits.

The use of formative assessment practices in larger systems embodies a belief at the heart of the missions of social profit organizations: an optimistic faith that things can change for the better. Let's end with some thoughts about change itself, on multiple levels.

10

Changing Our Minds—and Cultures

WHEN I ASK PRACTITIONERS WHAT GETS IN THE WAY of formative assessment work in social profit organizations, people generally cite two major forces: lack of time and resistance to change.

I have addressed the lack of time, which is a formidable obstacle but possible to overcome if an organization sticks with scheduling mission time long enough to get good at using it. It is the second impediment—resistance to change—that may get in the way of that happening. These two forces are obviously related: It may be that the *perceived* lack of time is an indicator of a very *real* resistance to change. But either way, resistance to change may be the more daunting obstacle to changing habits in the long run. Most organizations can put together a team to write a rubric or two, but then there will be the tendency to say, "Okay, rubric written, now let's get back to normal." What I am advocating is a new normal—which takes us into the realms of human nature and change itself.

— Confronting Change —

Social profit organizations are human organizations, and human beings are full of paradoxes. We are blessed with the ability to picture realities that do not yet exist, but if our minimal needs are met we are drawn to the status quo. We love ideas, but we prefer that they be our own if we are going to act upon them. We will join efforts against long odds if we believe our colleagues are by our side, but we will resist doing something simple and obvious if we feel we are being forced to do it. We admire the concept of collaborative efforts, but we instinctively protect our individual prerogatives.

How do you change human institutions? A widely used formula for change that dates back to the 1960s illustrates what it takes to overcome the power of resistance. The corresponding equation has been shown in different ways over the years, but it always has Resistance to Change (R) on one side and the factors necessary to override that resistance on the other. Widely known as the Beckhard model—named after Richard Beckhard, one of its popularizers—the formula looks like this:

$$\text{Dissatisfaction} \times \text{Vision} \times \text{First Steps} > \text{Resistance to Change}$$

Or, simply put:

$$D \times V \times F > R$$

Let's take a look at the left side of the equation. It includes:

- Vision (V)—a clear and compelling picture of what changes we would like to see in the future. This is what we will be *planning backward* from.
- First steps (F)—concrete, manageable action steps that lead toward the new vision. This is knowing how to begin, and what to do next.
- Dissatisfaction (D) with the status quo. Beckhard posits that unless the way things are is unacceptable to a good number of people, and particularly to people in power, change is unlikely.

I like the model for a few reasons. For one thing, it helps explain why so many glaring inequities and solvable problems go unattended for decades: People with wealth and political power and leverage over social and economic systems are not the ones who are dissatisfied. For another, it aligns with formative assessment thinking. When you measure what matters, assessment:

- Is a first step—*Are we measuring what matters? What would success look like?*—not something that happens at the end.
- Continuously improves and sharpens the vision: We know what we are planning backward from, and with each draft of the rubric, the picture is clearer and the bar is higher. Remember the server in chapter 5: *Good evening, Mr. Yingling. Welcome back.*
- Increases dissatisfaction with the status quo because it describes and clarifies the gap between current and desired performance, as an organization or as a society.
- Reduces resistance to change because we do it together. It is not *his* rubric; it is *our* rubric. Decisions do not come out of nowhere from the central office; they are hammered out together in mission time.

As I have thought about this change model over the years, I can't help but add a galvanizing element: leadership (L). Only leadership can create and sanction mission time; it is up to leaders to model the levels of honesty and collaboration and lack of defensiveness that formative assessment demands; it is up to leaders to create the spirit of ongoing learning that characterizes an assessment culture. So with all due respect to Beckhard, I would suggest that the formula should be: $L \times D \times V \times F > R$.

What do you think? Here's a good exercise for your group during mission time: Put a capital R on one side of an equation and then ask what you would need to have on the other side of the equation to be equal to or greater than this resistance. Come up with your own answer to this question: *What do we need to have in place to overcome resistance to change?*

But having a change model is only the beginning. I think there is still more we have to do to create assessment cultures. There is more we have to understand—together.

— Creating an Assessment Mind-Set —

If I were writing a rubric on Organizational Assessment Practices, here's what I would put at the next-to-highest level: organizations that understand the power of assessment to shape as well as judge performance, that are comfortable with the concept of planning backward, and that design and use rubrics to clarify what they are trying to do and get feedback on performance.

Just as with the Neighborhood Leadership Initiative instructions on asset mapping, or the GreenFaith ideas for worship services, or the Dodge Foundation's description of how to prepare for site visits, the next-to-highest level is very good. You nod and say, "That's impressive." But is it all we should aspire to? No. Let's think longer-term, and since the rubric invites us to do it, let's ask what it would *really* look like to get assessment right as social profit organizations.

For me the answer is clear: an assessment mind-set would be at the center of your organization's *culture*. Formative assessment would not be viewed as a project with time boundaries. These practices would not go away with a change of leadership on the staff or board. They would be part of your organizational DNA.

I think back to the question about what needs to be in our individual and collective long-term memories for this transformation to happen. When we need answers and guidance from the hidden depths of our own brains during our busy workdays, during staff and board meetings, and as we think about the futures of our organizations, what will be there to help us to build assessment cultures?

I have argued that certain *concepts* will need to be there— concepts like mission time, planning backward, and a rehabilitated view of feedback. I have argued that the *experience of rubric writing* with your colleagues should be there. I have suggested that certain *questions* will be there as well, posed regularly. The social sector as a whole has questions that inspire and test us: *What is the good life? What is the common good? What is effective philanthropy?* And organizations with assessment cultures do, too: *What does the world need from us? What does success look like? How do we know if we are being successful?* Finally, I would add an additional compo- nent—a shared and ever-increasing *knowledge base* about the field in which the organization works and its history, and about organiza- tions themselves and the ways human beings work together. This last body of literature is one we have to help one another discover.

Changing (as in developing and improving) our minds in this way and thus changing our organizational cultures, as I have said, requires leadership, on multiple levels. I would like to close with some unabashed coaching to three kinds of leaders in the social sector system. You might have fun yourselves during mission time by posing the following question and discussing it in small groups: *If you wanted to define and achieve what matters most to you and eventually build a culture that fostered ongoing learning, what advice would you give to: (1) executive directors; (2) board members; and (3) foundation officers?* Here are my answers:

— To Executive Directors/CEOs —

Signal that assessment work matters to you and to the organization. The chances that significant formative assessment work can happen without you are minimal. Particularly as your staff start to take more time for reflection about what matters most to them and begin to draft rubrics, some portion of the group will be looking at you and wondering, *Do we really have to do this? I'd like to get back to work,* or *Is this another fad from a workshop that I can outlast?* But if you model the idea that ongoing learning through formative assessment *is* the work, and that ongoing work in the world fuels that learning, they will understand they are part of a new system that requires, and rewards, their participation and best efforts.

Remember, you don't have to do it yourself. In a learning organization, the executive director sets a tone, an agenda, and expectations in the way a teacher does in a classroom. And one of the insights teachers have gained through recent discoveries in cognitive science is elegantly summarized by Terry Doyle in *Learner Centered Teaching*: "It is the one who does the work who does the learning."

There is growing recognition in educational circles, particularly in higher education, that *the teacher does too much of the work.* You can see why the lecture model persists: The lecturer is talking about something he or she loves, and the student simply needs to show up. But what about learning? The same pattern can occur in social sector organizations, where the executive director can take on the burden of every detail of decision making while staff wait for their "assignments."

If you want your board and staff to be learners, you need to be sure they have work to do. The approach to rubric writing I have described in chapters 5 and 6 and illustrated in chapters 7 through 9 is a framework for work that is, by design, about pursuing the aspects of the mission of the organization that matter most to them. Give them time to do it.

Help your staff and board though "the groan zone." Creating social profit requires both expansive, divergent thinking about possibilities and disciplined, convergent thinking about choices. Making choices can cause conflict, and busy social sector organizations—indeed, normal, healthy human beings—avoid conflict if they can. But if you help everyone understand that the "groan zone"[19] is a necessary part of resolving different perspectives and choosing among possible directions, people can handle it. They won't think something is wrong with them, or with you. They will understand the phrase *No pain, no gain* in the way that athletes do. They will consider the idea that if it is too easy, they are probably missing something. On the other side of the groan zone, staffs and boards of social profit organizations can come together around very specific, prioritized, often innovative actions that advance their mission and achieve their vision of success. The surest way to get there is through sufficient mission time designated for the task and the patient, optimistic leadership of an executive director.

Help your board and staff acquire a shared knowledge base. In the social sector, we tend to view professional development as something that happens away from work rather than at work and through work. We send people off to workshops or courses but don't provide any vehicle for incorporating their learning; rather, as I have said before, we find ways to deflect it so it won't slow us down or potentially disrupt our routines. But imagine the rich, ongoing conversation you can have with your colleagues if you ask: *What do we need to all understand about our field to help us define and enhance our role in it? What do we need to understand about organizations so that we can have a healthy one?*

My favorite approach is to set a very narrow boundary—a Foot-Long Bookshelf (see the appendix). What if whatever you put on that twelve-inch-long piece of shelving would be completely absorbed and fully understood by everyone in your organization? What would you put on the shelf? This discussion is a great use of mission time—after you have written your rubrics!

— To Board Members —

Be sure an assessment system exists. In Susan Stevens's remarkably helpful book *Nonprofit Lifecycles*, she uses the metaphor of a table to remind us that the mission and programs of an organization (the tabletop) must be supported by the four sturdy legs of management, governance, financial resources, and administrative systems. The board is responsible for the soundness of the whole table, but in my experience they tend to leave administrative systems—including an assessment system—to the administrators. Fair enough; board members do not need to get into the weeds of operations. But they have to be sure the staff is assessing the impact of external programs and the efficacy of internal structures and processes that support their work in the world. Board members don't have to *do* the assessing, but their thinking about strategy and policy should be informed by the assessing, and they should ask, *Are we measuring what matters?*

Model the practice by assessing yourself. The governance leg of the table will be strongest if the board is in the practice of asking, *What does success look like for us as a board? What do we mean when we say someone is doing a good job as a board member of this organization at this stage of its development?* There are many examples of board self-evaluation rubrics and questionnaires available on the Internet and in publications by organizations that support the social sector. But for reasons I have already explained, I advocate writing your own rubric. Use local language and examples. Own it.

Avoid the trap of underinvesting in organizational development. A 2013 TED talk by Dan Pallotta titled "The Way We Think About Charity Is Dead Wrong,"[20] has been viewed almost three million times in its first ten months online. According to Pallotta, "Our social problems are gigantic in scale, our organizations are tiny up against them—and we have beliefs that keep them tiny." He says social sector organizations still tend to view mission-driven work as a calling rather than an occupation that deserves compensation for excellent performance, so salaries in the sector are modest. They view marketing and advertising as more appropriate for toothpaste than for ideas. They are risk-averse because they do not want to be seen as wasting donated money, let alone public money, and risk capital is generally unavailable to them. They expect quick, measurable results so they can make a case in annual funding cycles, so are loathe to build physical or relational infrastructures that will take years to deliver. Only a board can set policies that can counter these beliefs and forces.

Again, this is why we must change our terminology from *nonprofit*—which only signifies it is not a business—and *NGO*—which only signifies it is not a government agency—to *social profit* organizations. Social profit is worth investing in.

— To Foundation Officers —

The importance of individual donors notwithstanding, you are the ones whose attitudes, strategies, processes, and relationships with your grantees define organized philanthropy, and the system runs on philanthropy. Much of the enlightened thinking about evaluation and measurement has come from foundations. Even so, like the rest of the social sector, foundations are diverse and the field is fragmented, thus I offer these thoughts.

Be sure to respond to (and promote) the right measures. Of course foundations want the organizations they support to be both efficient and effective. To me, the biggest mistake we can make in this area is to assume that the lower the overhead costs, the more effective the organization. There is a big difference between efficiency—which is a very good idea up to a point—and effectiveness—which can be compromised when efficiency becomes an end in itself. The pressure on organizations to minimize the amount of money they spend on their own capacity to deliver social profit is counterproductive. The real end is social profit, and that is what we should be measuring.

Likewise, when measuring impact, we have to be careful not to elevate "numbers served" as the primary measure of success. Of course foundations want to affect as many people as possible; so do the social profit organizations. But those organizations know there is a dramatic difference between seeming to serve and actually serving individuals and communities in need. I have had social profit leaders tell me that they have had to compromise or even dismantle their most effective programs because of the push from foundations to serve more people—without any additional funds to increase the organization's capacity to serve them well.

What does serving well mean? That answer is at the heart of serious, ongoing self-assessment efforts in the social sector. It is what people will describe when you ask them what success looks like for them in fulfilling their missions, and even more it is what they will describe when you ask them what success *really* looks like. The definition of serving well depends on a number of local factors: historical, cultural, social, economic, environmental. Community-based organizations in particular understand the subtleties of context, and those understandings are reflected in their formative assessment efforts. Thus it is important for foundation officers to be open to and welcoming of those efforts.

Respect local measures. I spent two years as chair of the Council of New Jersey Grantmakers, which had 111 member organizations at the time. From that position, I urged my colleagues to think about what we were asking our grantee organizations to do when we asked them to report back to us in multiple ways, on our own evaluation forms. I said then and still believe that any single foundation, or group of foundations, cannot devise an evaluation form that will fit the diverse and subtle work of multiple grantees.

The best foundation evaluation systems ask organizations to be more formal and systematic in their *self*-assessment efforts. These helpful systems begin with the guidelines for applying, which ask organizations to address in their proposals what they are planning backward from, what their criteria for success are, and what success will look like. They then build a reporting form around these answers. It is a way of teaching the principles of the early chapters of this book. But to the grantee, it may feel like they are simply responding to the requirements of a particular donor rather than shifting how they think about assessment. What if foundations took it one step farther and gave up directly assessing the work of individual grantees, and instead evaluated how well their grantees assessed *their own* work?

Consider teaching your grantee organizations how to better self-assess. Many foundations provide technical assistance to their grantees, either directly or indirectly. It makes a lot of sense to back up big mission-based investments with relatively modest investments in the well-being and effectiveness of those who are acting as their agents in bringing about positive change in the world. My argument is that there is great bang for the buck in helping grantees adopt the mind-set, and eventually the culture, of self-evaluation. I do not think there is a single point of leverage as powerful, and it does not need new equipment or technical expertise. It needs time and a frame of mind—and donors who respect the results.

—— To Everyone: Create Your —— Own Assessment Systems

Let's go back to the generic executive director, board member, and foundation officer we met in chapter 1, the ones I said deserved a better assessment system. Remember that the executive director was working late in the night before a board meeting, completing a proposal to a local foundation, answering a question about how she would measure her outcomes, and using the metrics she had used before. She sensed that those numbers missed the most important part of the story, but felt she couldn't report on the organization's biggest achievement, because she would have to talk about learning from a big mistake. Remember that the new board member of her organization was en route to the meeting. He had run out of time to look at the preparatory materials, but knew the major points would be repeated at the meeting. In other words, his expectation was that the meeting would be a report to board members, nothing more. Remember that the foundation officer who eventually received the director's proposal compared the numbers served from one year to another, and wondered if that reflected real change or not. Recall, too, what that officer thought: *This feels more like a dance than an evaluation.*

In the spirit of "the one who does the work does the learning," I'll ask *you* how you would picture this executive director, board member, and foundation officer if they were in a new and different assessment system of their own devising. How would the story change for:

- The executive director writing the grant proposal?
- The new board member driving to the board meeting?
- The foundation officer reading the grant proposal and the report on the previous year's grant?

Here's what I picture: The executive director would be attaching qualitative assessment rubrics created by her staff and board to the application. She would note that the rubric on "Relationships," which prompted revised job descriptions and new training for the staff, seems to have had a dramatic positive effect on the metrics she usually reports on. She would explain how the visioning process to create the rubrics had caused the organization to end one program and begin another. She would summarize the results of their regular mission time question: *What are we learning from our mistakes?* She would explain how the formative assessment work revealed that the organization does not have the capacity to affect what matters most to them, so they have reached out in partnership to two other organizations, and they need the foundation's help in funding the process of creating a rubric in common.

The board member would be looking forward to describing his recent activities as a "community ambassador," one of the areas on the board rubric about "Roles and Contributions" that had played such a valuable part in his orientation to the board. He would also be looking forward to discussing the first chapter of *Switch: How to Change Things When Change Is Hard*, which had been sent to all board members three weeks before the meeting (see the appendix). The board role of "Learner" on the rubric had surprised him at first, but it had quickly become his favorite part of being on the board; the discussions seemed to be helping the organization a lot, and he was learning things he could use in his job and at home as well.

The foundation officer would be appreciating how honest the proposal is about challenges and difficulties, and how clear it is about what the organization is trying to do. She would be thrilled to see that board giving has doubled since the board rubric increased their engagement so dramatically. She would be thinking, *I like how their rubric identified that it's not how many people showed up for their workshop but whether people were using the material six months later that matters to them. So they designed a way to get that information, which led to a monthly meeting for ongoing mutual support. Of course it makes sense for us to fund that; it's a great return on our investment.* She might see that they had identified communications as their biggest weakness at this point and think, *I should get them together with our other grantee with about the same-sized budget that just wrote a new communications plan.*

Possible? Yes. Versions of the above scenes are already happening and becoming more frequent. You may already be among the examples. But if not, or if you still have a way to go, think about this line in *Learner Centered Teaching*, attributed to L. B. Resnick: "What you assess is what you get. If you don't test it, you won't get it."

Transfer this understanding to the social sector, and you understand the purpose—and the beauty—of formative assessment. The steps are simple:

- Decide what you want and envision it.
- If you can't measure the success you envision in numbers, describe it—with your colleagues in a rubric.
- Plan backward from that vision of success the rubric helps you clarify.
- Revise the rubric based on using it, and on your ongoing learning, and on new demands in a changing world.
- Assess your progress toward your vision.

Many of you will get there. All of you will come closer than if you had not tried to embrace assessment practices that allowed you to define with care and imagination the social profit you exist to produce. And all the rest of us will be grateful for your efforts.

AFTERWORD

In October 2007, I attended a gathering of environmental leaders at The Aspen Institute in Colorado, under the auspices of Yale's School of Forestry and Environmental Studies (FES). The conference had a New Age title, "Towards a New Consciousness," but it was a mainstream group of close to one hundred environmental elders in the room, mostly men, almost all white, who were acknowledging that the ways they had been thinking and talking about global environmental threats were not working. The estimable dean of FES, Gus Speth, led off with a presentation about the severity of our linked social and environmental crises that had people close to weeping. We definitely, even desperately, needed cheering up.

Then the author and green business entrepreneur Paul Hawken did just that. He did not supply a new consciousness but he did give us the next best thing—a new metaphor. Presenting the thesis of his then recently published book, *Blessed Unrest*, he claimed the largest social justice movement in the history of the world was under way, with literally millions of people and organizations with social missions responding to the ills and threats of our time, and he said he believed this movement was largely invisible, because it was so fragmented, leaderless, and bottom-up in nature. He likened these numerous, varied, mission-driven responses to human antibodies that appear when needed to fight disease. In this metaphor, suddenly there is hope; it is as if human society and the earth itself have an immune system.

Since I was running a foundation, the metaphor suggested a new way of looking at grantees to me. I began to see the various organizations working on arts education, on social justice for immigrants, on clean water issues, on responsible media, on the creation of new works for the stage, on providing services for the elderly, as separate parts of the same impulse for a safer, fairer, cleaner, more joyful world. They were social profit "antibodies." And I went home with the conviction that a place-based foundation should do everything in its power to make these health-seeking antibodies stronger themselves, then connect them and their efforts and impacts wherever possible for a cumulative effect. This book is an extension of that impulse.

While I love the formal cross-sectoral and multi-organizational connections described in chapter 9, I am heartened by the idea that organizations do not have to know one another for their efforts to be connected. The child protected from asthma by one social profit organization is able to go to school and meet the inspiring artist sent by another; on her way home she can stop at the urban supermarket created by another and then join her parents at family night at the theater sponsored by another still. The antibodies are at work, and the wellness, the social profit, is growing. It is another way of looking at what poet Adrienne Rich called "the meaning of *we*."

Please join me in another experiment in the power of *we*. I invite all of you who adopt formative assessment principles and practices to share what you are learning and inspire one another by going to the website www.socialprofithandbook.com and uploading rubrics and commentary. We will see where the learning takes us.

In the meantime, try a rubric with your colleagues—and your clients. That small change can make a big difference.

APPENDIX:
The Foot-Long Bookshelf

I HAVE SUGGESTED that building a shared knowledge base is key to "changing the minds" of everyone in your organization, in the most positive and collegial way. Here is a question for you. *If you had only a single, foot-long piece of bookshelf, and the books you put on it would be instantly known and well understood by the staff and board of your organization, what would you put on the shelf?*

Some will be about the field in which you operate: health; the arts; education; the environment; social services. I urge you to propose those books and essays (and blogs and videos) to one another. It is also helpful to have a shared vocabulary and conceptual framework for organizational life and for the systems in which you find yourselves. Here, too, I urge you to suggest candidates for that precious foot of shelf space.

In the meantime, let me tell you about some of the books I would suggest for any social nonprofit's foot-long shelf. All of them relate to building an assessment culture and some actually shed light on one another, as I'll explain below.

Nonprofit Lifecycles by Susan Stevens

The first book I would propose for your shelf would be *Nonprofit Lifecycles* by Susan Stevens. At the Dodge Foundation, we used to buy this book by the carton to hand out to our grantees. Stevens presents a stage-based approach to understanding organizational development, identifying and explaining the following stages:

- **Idea.** This is when someone sees a need in the world and thinks it may require an organized response, even a new organization. Most ideas do not actually become organizations; the person may have another idea, or get back to work, or go to dinner. But some ideas are too compelling to drop; they become the inspiration for a new 501(c)3 organization, which begins life as a . . .
- **Start-up.** This stage is what Stevens calls the labor of love. Nothing is formal. The board consists of the founder's brother, college roommate, and next-door neighbor. The task is to become known in the world and recognized for the potential social profit the group can deliver. Many organizations go right to the terminal stage from start-up, but some take hold and move to . . .
- **Growth.** This is a long stage for many organizations. It is where they decide who they are, and try to get finances under control and systems formalized for the long haul. This stage contains a major challenge—the transition from the founder to new leadership; the arrival of that moment is as predictable as adolescence is to human development, and as potentially risky. Growth organizations can go into decline; they can go out of business; but some of them move to . . .
- **Maturity.** This is the stage organizations reach if successive generations of staff and board leadership have created a clear sense of purpose and the capacity to deliver social

profit consistently. Systems are stable and sustainable. Even so, even the best organizations go into . . .

- **Decline.** Like illness to a human, decline can come at any time and is to be periodically expected. The key is to recognize it and deal with it, which leads to . . .
- **Turnaround.** Here an organization addresses whatever needs addressing and returns to healthy development. Or if the decline cannot be halted, the final stage is . . .
- **Terminal.** Not much elaboration needed here.

My purpose here is not to summarize the subtleties of the stages so much as to suggest that using the model as an ongoing diagnostic tool fits hand in glove with the creation of an assessment culture. It also very powerfully sets the *non-defensive tone* so essential for an assessment culture. In the absence of the life cycles perspective, when things go wrong, you ask whose fault it is. With the life cycles perspective, when things go wrong, you say, "Of course we have this problem to deal with. It is a predictable challenge of our stage of development." What a relief, particularly to overworked executive directors, who usually blame themselves.

Stevens points out it is not always easy to pinpoint where you are on the developmental arc, because the line of that arc is more like a rainbow, with separate strands for programs, management, governance, financial resources, and administrative systems. Rarely are all these elements aligned, or developing at the same pace.

Arts organizations, for example, are well known for having program development get out ahead of administrative systems. A young dance company might present a breathtaking performance, but behind the scenes they don't have a copy machine and have forgotten to withhold income taxes. An experimental theater might present an important new play, but the playbill was folded at midnight by board members drinking wine at the artistic director's apartment. So in an assessment culture, the life-cycles model provides some regular questions: *Where are we? How do we get as aligned as possible? What's coming next, and how do we prepare for it?*

As I noted in chapter 10, Stevens uses the metaphor of a table to represent how important it is not to neglect the development of any of the strands in that rainbow. She imagines an organization's mission as a flowering plant sitting on a tabletop of programs that support the mission. Supporting the programs are the four "table legs" of management, governance, financial resources, and administrative systems. You can see what happens if any of the table legs is shorter than the others: The table wobbles. If any of the legs stops developing appropriately and gets really short, the table will tip and the mission will crash—terminal. In an assessment culture, we periodically ask: *How's our table?* This simple question can lead to important observations:

- *I'm not sure we are all clear on what the mission is that we are supporting.*
- *I don't think our financial resources leg is strong enough to hold the breadth of programs we are offering.*
- *I think our board was perfect for the last stage of our development, but not for the one we are in; that leg is getting shaky.*
- *We've grown to the point where we have to bolster the systems leg with a communications policy, and more capacity in this area.*
- *The staff leg is coming unglued; we are all too tired and need to take better care of ourselves.*

You will have your own observations based on your own organization. Imagine sitting with your colleagues in unhurried mission time and asking, *How's our table?*

Change by Design by Tim Brown

Another book I would nominate for your shared bookshelf is Tim Brown's *Change by Design*. Brown is president and CEO of IDEO, an international design and innovation consulting firm, and he argues persuasively that design thinking is not reserved for architects and landscape gardeners, or those working on product teams at Apple or Gucci. IDEO's clients tend to be for-profit businesses and governments, but the applications of their concepts in the social sector are profound.

Let's imagine you have your metaphorical table from *Nonprofit Lifecycles* in reasonable balance. Your assessment thinking about ensuring your own capacity to pursue a clear and important mission has paid off. There remains the hard work of pursuing that mission in a complex and changing world. One way to approach that work is to think of ourselves as designers.

My favorite notion in his book can be represented by a Venn diagram with three intersecting circles. Design thinkers are searching for the sweet spot in the middle of the drawing where three elements/conditions overlap: desirability; viability; and feasibility.

Viability means, *Can we afford it?* Feasibility means, *Is it possible?* Let's note that in the social profit world, feasibility has technical, political, and cultural dimensions; it can get complicated.

Brown argues that good design is rooted in the dimension of *desirability*, and I think this is one of the lessons social profit staff and board members can take from his book. In a sector starved for resources and confronted with daunting social ills, we can find ourselves slipping into the part of the diagram where *viability* and *feasibility* overlap, just outside the *desirability* circle. The test is how we answer the question, *Why are you doing it that way?* If we find ourselves answering, *Because that's what we could afford* or *Because that was our only option*, instead of an answer based on mission language, we have slipped out of the zone where the three design elements overlap.

I think the Venn diagram is also helpful when we think about the top column of our rubrics. By definition, what we describe at the top of the rubric is desirable—it expresses what we most desire for our organizations and our impact in the world. But the top of the rubric—what we envision and aspire to—may not be feasible or viable. It probably isn't.

This gives us a new take on where to focus our creative efforts. It is a subtle but important difference to believe that creativity lies not in imagining what we want to have happen, but rather in making what we want to happen become possible and affordable. Assessment cultures follow this pattern: They begin with what it looks like in the world if their mission is fulfilled. Then they apply design thinking to the other two dimensions.

Another very helpful concept for social profit organizations in Brown's book is his point that design involves alternating periods of divergent and convergent thinking—periods of producing a range of ideas and possible choices, followed by periods of narrowing down ideas and making choices among the possibilities you have generated. One divergent/convergent cycle follows another. You imagine choices of direction, then you decide on one. Having decided on one, you imagine various ways of going about whatever you have chosen, then decide on a way. Having decided on a way, you brainstorm on who should know about it, then narrow down the list. It goes on.

Design teams become very good at knowing where they are in this cyclical process. But social profit staffs and particularly boards do not customarily spend their time working together as design thinkers. So discussions can become strained if one person is in a divergent stage of thinking and another is looking at the clock and thinking, *Let's wrap this up*. A facilitator can help, but how often do you have that luxury? Better that you adopt the mental model of an undulating series of divergent and convergent cycles and decide together which part of the cycle you are in.

Facilitator's Guide to Participatory Decision-Making by Sam Kaner

"Decide together" is simple enough to say, but hard to do. Another indicator of an assessment culture, right up there with planning backward, understanding life cycles, and thinking like designers, is making decisions in as participatory and transparent a way as possible.

When Tim Brown talks so logically of cycles of divergent and convergent thinking, he makes it seem as if you can blow a whistle and say, "Time to converge!" If only it were that easy. The problem is that if you have made time for thinking that is actually divergent and encouraged that thinking (commonly referred to as "thinking outside the box"), you will have multiple perspectives and possibilities on the table that will make convergence a challenge. Thus another understanding that I think assessment cultures should embrace is captured in Sam Kaner's admirable guide, the one I referred to in my advice to executive directors in chapter 10. It is to expect a "groan zone" before you can converge and come to closure.

What an important concept to understand—that reconciling different perspectives and points of view, and weighing the benefits of possible actions, is groan-inducing. It is not that there is an inadequate leader, or that the group doesn't get along, or that the group has a bad habit of talking everything to death. No, it is that you have done enough divergent thinking to get into the groan zone.

How do you get out of it? Here is where it pays to be an assessment culture. You will have scheduled sufficient mission time to work things through. You will have identified your core values and described desirable outcomes—the tops of your rubrics—and they will serve as touchstones for decision making. You will be used to discussing the relative merits of ideas rather than choosing sides based on personal loyalties. You will have a theory of change that will move you toward convergence. And you will not resent being in the groan zone; you will expect it, even welcome it. You will say to one another, "We must be getting somewhere because I am getting uncomfortable. We are obviously in the groan zone." Sometimes divergent perspectives can be combined into a third and stronger alternative. Sometimes, you just have to choose. People in an assessment culture will always give the first a try, and they will know when it's time for the second.

It is helpful to apply the design-thinking paradigm to the idea of participatory decision making. If you wrote a rubric on the topic, you would not put participation of every staff and board member on every decision at the top of the rubric. You might instead write something like, "Staff and board members are clear about when and how decisions are made. There are mechanisms for input from all interested parties before decisions are made. Staff and board understand the difference between strategic and operational decisions and understand each other's roles and responsibilities in making these decisions. All members of the organization feel appropriately informed and engaged in key decisions related to mission, organizational values and identity, and strategic goals and objectives. Decisions on important matters are reviewed periodically by the whole organization and refreshed in response to changing circumstances, because time has been allotted for that task."

Desirable? Yes, if that's what you have decided. Viable? Yes, this is not a matter of money. Feasible? Yes, with good leadership.

Switch by Dan and Chip Heath

When I was still president of the Geraldine R. Dodge Foundation, a number of the executive directors from the organizations we were funding and I got together for a series of seminar-style discussions about some essays and poems we had read in common. When I asked for a vote at the end on the single most useful reading, they chose the first chapter of *Switch: How to Change Things When Change Is Hard.*

The Heath brothers have been generous in providing downloadable sections of the book and other resources through their website www.switchthebook.com. Even so, their argument is elegantly compressed into an image—a three-part metaphor for thinking about change: a human *Rider*, sitting on the back of an *Elephant*, proceeding (or not) down a *Path*.

The rider represents the intellectual dimension of our decision making and the elephant the emotional; note their relative sizes. The path is the environment in which we attempt to move toward change. Change can be very difficult because the rider may overthink the journey and be overwhelmed with choices; she may not know which direction to head in. The elephant is comfortable where he is, and would just as soon sit there. The path may not be easy to see, and it may be crowded with obstacles.

So the Heaths recommend that as we contemplate change, we consider three strategies, singly or in combination depending on the circumstances. We may have to direct the rider and be clear about where we want to go and what the first step in that direction looks like. We may have to motivate the elephant with a sense of passion and purpose. We may have to shape the path toward our destination by removing obstacles that currently block our progress, or widen the way through new resources or partnerships or policies.

Switch is full of examples, and you may be applying the metaphor already yourselves. Let's apply it to the task of building an assessment culture, a hard change to be sure. You know I have advocated shaping the path first, through identifying and protecting mission time. There are other environmental factors to consider: a comfortable meeting room with good air and light; the shared bookshelf; good food . . . wait, I hear the elephant stirring.

But that's only motivating him to get to the meeting. Motivating the elephant to change when change is hard always takes us back to mission. If the elephant feels that people will be better served, that the values he holds dear will be advanced, he will move with great power; don't get in his way. So making the case to colleagues for embracing formative assessment is rarely about actual measuring; it is about defining what matters. It is about the V (vision) part of Beckhard's change model. The rider is motivated by the mission, too, in a more cerebral way, but she needs an assignment. So take what Beckhard would call a first step (the F in his change model): a SWOT exercise; or writing the first paragraph of that magazine article you would be planning backward from; or drafting a rubric based on key words in your mission statement.

One of the actions the Heaths suggest is to "build habits," because then the rider doesn't even have to think about where to go. The path is shaped by the habits. That for me is what we are doing when we build an assessment culture: habitually applying concepts, posing key questions, and turning our shared learning into right action.

The Human Side of School Change
by Robert Evans

Another writer who sheds light on how difficult it is to bring about institutional change is the psychologist Robert Evans. In his book, he explains that people experience change, no matter how sensible it is, in four ways:

- As **loss**, since the patterns of our lives form our sense of identity. When the patterns change, we actually mourn.
- As a feeling of **incompetence**, since we know how to do it the old way and not the new.

- As **confusion**, since when anything in a system changes, there are always unexpected consequences; we tweak Tuesday and suddenly something is different on Thursday.
- As **conflict**, since change in a workplace can serve as an excuse to bring out long-held grievances; it *seems* as if we are arguing about some aspect of our new approach, but what is sometimes happening is that years ago one person got the parking place, or the office, that another one wanted—and now the nagging frustration has an outlet.

It is helpful not only for those leading change but also for everyone experiencing it to understand these otherwise hidden psychological forces. Such understanding helps us answer that most basic of assessment questions: *What's going on?*

Leadership and the New Science
by Margaret Wheatley

We need to save room on the Foot-Long Bookshelf for some books that talk about systems, since building an assessment culture is equivalent to creating a system for ongoing learning and wise application of that learning. This book was originally written for a business audience; it was named the Business Book of the Year in 1992 when it first came out. But many social sector leaders have appreciated Wheatley's application of twentieth-century scientific discoveries to systems thinking, and she adds a couple of key questions to the list of those we should habitually ask ourselves if we are going to develop an assessment culture.

Wheatley notes that twentieth-century science teaches us that the world is not as orderly and bound by physical laws as we once thought. If you think that Newton got it right and the universe unfolds logically, think again. Citing chaos theory, fractals, and the like, Wheatley observes that while a larger system finds an order, things are quite unpredictable at the local level. Suddenly we begin to understand why our best-laid plans often go awry. A key board member is sick for a particular meeting. It rains on the day of your fund-raising golf event. A parking lot meeting reverses the direction you thought the group had decided.

When I first encountered Wheatley's book, I remember a feeling of liberation: *You mean I don't have to try to control things anymore?* To some extent that is correct, though responsibility has not gone away. It has shifted. Instead of focusing on specific planned outcomes, we should be focusing on the health of our system.

Systems will find an order—but will the order be more or less beneficial to more or fewer people? We have some influence over that if not full control. According to Wheatley, systems find their best order when two factors are present: good information and good relationships. If you think about your organization as a system, the relevance is striking—and so is the argument for building an assessment culture.

One of the ongoing assessment questions we should be asking is, *Do we have the information we need?* Some of it is internal and is worked out in mission time: *What are we trying to do? Who's responsible for what? What indicators of success are we looking for?* And some of the information we need is external; it is data that may or may not come easily. If it does not come easily, we must design how to get it. Once we have good information, we need good relationships, internally and externally, to decide what to do with it. It is another argument for increased transparency and inclusiveness. In the old model of leadership, information is power. In the newer model Wheatley describes, information is energy to a system that is finding the right order.

Good information as energy to a system, interpreted and applied by people in good relationship to one another, with a shared sense of purpose. It is a nice image. With full acknowledgment that I have beaten this particular dead horse past recognition,

I'll observe that no organization could act on this vision without mission time.

The Six Secrets of Change by Michael Fullan

I had taught poetry for years before coming to the Dodge Foundation, but paradoxically it took leaving the classroom for me to become more immersed in poetry as a living art, thanks to the foundation's remarkable biennial poetry festival. More than ever, I was impressed by the characteristic of poetry that separates it from the other arts—an extraordinary power of compression. Single words or lines or images or phrases in poems can carry a weight of meaning and emotion that can make your jaw drop. In the thrall of a great poet, you think and feel, *No one could have said it better in any other way.*

I recently had that feeling in relation to the themes of my book, though the "poetry" came from an unlikely source: a scholarly work on leadership and organizational change by University of Toronto professor emeritus Michael Fullan. In his book *The Six Secrets of Change*, he advocates for "purposeful peer interaction and learning in relation to results."[21]

Here, I thought, was language as compressed as an Emily Dickinson poem. *Purposeful peer interaction and learning in relation to results.* It struck me as the nine-word answer to the question of how to put into effect all the lessons I have tried to present in these pages.

- **Purposeful** reminds us that everything is grounded in mission, and that time spent clarifying why our organizations exist comes back later to save us time and spare us confusion.
- **Peer interaction** can't happen unless organizational structures, habits, schedules, and physical space allow it to happen; all these are choices available to us.

- **Learning in relation to results** can't happen unless we have figured out what results matter to us. Here is the case for a focus on formative assessment practices designed to improve the work, not judge it.

All of you have visions of results to strive for: in assessment practices; in board policies and practices of all kinds; in strategic planning and financial management; in the relationship between board chair and executive director; in fund-raising. What Fullan's phrase does is put those results where they belong—not as vague hopes but as specific goals, not as things to talk and think about when we pause from our work but as the concepts that should animate our daily work. As Fullan further comments, "Successful organizations see working and learning to work better as one and the same."

Fullan's words may not be as immortal as "Out, out brief candle . . . ,"[22] but organizations that follow his advice are likely to be around a long time. With the touchstone of clear purpose, with the practice of protecting time for peer interaction, and with the focus of that interaction on results that matter, those organizations are more likely to perform—and adapt—in ways that advance their missions.

The sixth and final "secret" Fullan presents is "Systems Learn." Exactly. They do if we set them up with clarity of purpose, a welcoming spirit of transparency, a sense of humor for human foibles, and a faith that if we habitually define and strive to achieve social profit, we can build a better world.

NOTES

1. The phrase *social profit organization* comes up whenever and wherever people are seeking a better name than *nonprofit* to describe organizations in the social sector. One of the best arguments for the designation may be found in Claire Gaudiani's essay in *The Chronicle of Philanthropy*, July 26, 2007, titled "Let's Put the 'Nonprofit' Out of Business." Gaudiani likes a hyphen, as in *social-profit organization*, but I prefer to let *profit* stand as a noun that requires an adjective.

2. In *America the Possible*, Gus Speth argues that we need to shift American investments from their dominant preference for earning financial returns to earning large social and environmental profits. He writes, "The capital allocation process has become far removed from institutions that serve the public interest and is instead dominated by institutions and individuals seeking only to maximize profits." How much money is out there "seeking high financial and low social returns"? Speth cites an estimate from 2006 of $190 trillion. See James Gustave Speth, *America the Possible: Manifesto for a New Economy* (New Haven, CT: Yale University Press, 2012), pp. 119–25.

3. See Sadhu Johnson, Steven S. Nicholas, and Julia Parzen, *The Guide to Greening Cities* (Washington, DC: Island Press, 2013), for success stories. In late 2014, the following

websites are also excellent resources for understanding urban sustainability efforts and finding descriptions of specific achievements: www.iclei.org (Local Governments for Sustainability); www.usdn.org (Urban Sustainability Directors Network); and www.www.sustainablecities institute.org (Nation League of Cities Sustainable Cities Institute).

4. Quoted in The Glossary of Educational Reform, an online resource created by the Great Schools Partnership, www. edglossary.org, which I accessed in September 2014. Paul Black is one of the authors (with Chris Harrison, Clare Lee, Bethan Marshall, and Dylan Wiliam) of *Assessment for Learning: Putting It into Practice* (New York, NY, and Maidenhead, UK: Open University Press, 2003).

5. From Daniel J. Levitin, *The Organized Mind: Thinking Straight in the Age of Information Overload* (New York: Dutton, 2014), p. 6.

6. From *The State of Nonprofit America*, 2nd edition, edited by Lester Salamon (Washington, DC: Brookings Institution Press, in collaboration with the Aspen Institute, 2002). The size of the nonprofit sector is described in Lester Salamon's overview essay, "The Resilient Sector: The Future of Nonprofit America."

7. Jean-francois Rischard's book *High Noon: 20 Global Problems, 20 Years to Solve Them* (New York: Basic Books, 2002) does a particularly good job of explaining how nation-states are not equipped to respond to problems that are multinational or global in scope. His solution—to appoint teams to work on each problem whose members, whatever their prior affiliations and expertise, see themselves as representing humankind—is not far removed from what we can imagine a more united and coordinated social profit sector accomplishing. It is a little daunting to think about the time frame implied in his subtitle.

8. The concept that Gross National Happiness (GNH) would be a better measure of success and progress than Gross National Product (GNP) or Gross Domestic Product (GDP) has been pioneered by the country of Bhutan and is being explored around the world. The US center (GNHUSA) is in my home state of Vermont. The goal is to build a national movement, and I would say its infrastructure is already in place: the civic sector, devoted to social rather than financial profit.

9. The poem is available on numerous poetry websites, some with commentary. It was originally published in Adrienne Rich, *Dark Fields of the Republic* (New York: W. W. Norton, 1995).

10. I owe this elegant insight to a breakfast conversation on September 11, 2014, with Antony Bugg-Levine, CEO of the Nonprofit Finance Fund and co-author (with Jed Emerson) of *Impact Investing: Transforming How We Make Money While Making a Difference* (San Francisco: Jossey-Bass, 2011).

11. From Michael Fullan's *Change Leader: Learning to Do What Matters Most* (San Francisco: Jossey-Bass, 2013), chapter 6.

12. Described in much greater detail in the essay "Accountability in the Nonprofit Sector," by Kevin P. Kearns, which is chapter 16 of *The State of Nonprofit America*, 2nd edition, mentioned above.

13. This quote is widely attributed to Einstein and sometimes rendered, "Not everything that can be counted counts. Not everything that counts can be counted." The website Quote Investigator (www.quoteinvestigator.com), which I accessed on September 15, 2014, suggests crediting William Bruce Cameron instead, from his 1963 text *Informal Sociology: A Casual Introduction to Sociological Thinking* (New York: Random House), p. 13. If you search for the quote on the Internet, you may surface a funny doctored photograph of Einstein at a blackboard, holding a piece of chalk and

writing, "Not everything that counts can be counted, and not everything that can be . . . wait! what? I don't think that was ever written on my blackboard."

When I think about our inclination to measure things, I am also reminded of a lovely poem by Robert Frost, "Choose Something Like a Star," which I commend to the reader. The poem examines the assumption that to know something as specifically and scientifically as possible is to understand it better. In the end, the star "asks of us a certain height," which, for me, is just what the missions of social profit organizations do.

14. This quick summary of how the brain works is drawn from Daniel T. Willingham's *Why Don't Children Like School?* (San Francisco: Jossey-Bass, 2009), pp. 13–14.

15. This is just one of the mantras Grant Wiggins has offered to several generations of teachers. His seminal works, the ones that most influenced me, were *Assessing Student Performance: Exploring the Purpose and Limits of Testing* (San Francisco: Jossey-Bass, 1993) and *Educative Assessment: Designing Assessments to Inform and Improve Student Performance* (San Francisco: Jossey-Bass, 1998).

16. This particular example comes from the website Copian: Connecting Canadians in Learning (http://en.copian.ca), accessed in October 2014. In their words: "The word 'Copian' is derived from the Latin word 'copia' meaning abundance, which speaks to our abundance of resources, expertise and experience, and the numerous benefits learners accumulate as a result of improved skills. In the spirit of a charitable, non-profit organization, Copian focuses its efforts on providing information and knowledge-sharing services free of charge to the literacy and workplace essential skills community."

17. My essay pursuing this idea with seven grantees of the Dodge Foundation is included in *The Coming Transformation: Values to Sustain Human and Natural Communities*, edited

by Stephen R. Kellert and James Gustave Speth (New Haven, CT: Yale School of Forestry and Environmental Studies, 2010).

18. At the time of this writing, October 2014, sources include www.noffn.org, www.wholecommunities.org, www.hunger freecommunities.org, and www.seattle.gov/neighborhoods. Entering "Whole Measures CFS" into a search engine in the future should lead to these and/or other sources. The *Stories from the Field* companion piece is available on the Whole Communities website.

19. The phrase is self-explanatory, which is one of its benefits. It comes from Sam Kaner et al., *Facilitator's Guide to Participatory Decision-Making* (San Francisco: Jossey-Bass, 2014), which I admire at some length in the appendix.

20. In October 2014, the talk is accessed at the following web address: http://www.ted.com/talks/dan_pallotta_the_way _we_think_about_charity_is_dead_wrong?language=en.

21. From Michael Fullan, *The Six Secrets of Change* (San Francisco: Jossey-Bass, 2008), p. 11.

22. Many of you will recognize this image as a line from Shakespeare's *Macbeth*, from the same speech that gave William Faulkner his title for *The Sound and the Fury*. I like to contrast Macbeth's despairing reference to life as a "brief candle" with the following lines from George Bernard Shaw (accessed at www.elise.com/quotes in October 2014), which capture the spirit of those who patiently, consistently, and joyfully pursue social profit: "I am of the opinion that my life belongs to the whole community, and as long as I live it is my privilege to do for it whatever I can ... Life is no 'brief candle' for me. It is a sort of splendid torch which I have got hold of for the moment, and I want to make it burn as brightly as possible before handing it on to future generations."

BIBLIOGRAPHY

Brown, Tim. *Change by Design: How Design Thinking Transforms Organizations and Inspires Innovation.* New York: HarperBusiness, 2009.

Covey, Stephen R. *The 7 Habits of Highly Effective People: Powerful Lessons in Personal Change.* New York: Simon and Schuster, 2013 (25th Anniversary edition).

Doyle, Terry. *Learner Centered Teaching: Putting the Research on Learning into Practice.* Sterling, VA: Stylus Publishing, 2011.

Evans, Robert. *The Human Side of School Change: Reform, Resistance, and the Real-Life Problems of Innovation.* San Francisco: Jossey-Bass, 2001.

Fleishman, Joel. *The Foundation: A Great American Secret.* New York: Public Affairs, 2007.

Fullan, Michael. *The Six Secrets of Change: What the Best Leaders Do to Help Their Organizations Survive and Thrive.* San Francisco: Jossey-Bass, 2011.

Hawken, Paul. *Blessed Unrest: How the Largest Movement in the World Came into Being and Why No One Saw It Coming.* New York: Viking Penguin, 2007.

Heath, Dan and Chip. *Switch: How to Change Things When Change Is Hard.* New York: Broadway Books, 2010.

Kaner, Sam, et al. *Facilitator's Guide to Participatory Decision-Making.* Hoboken, NJ: Jossey-Bass, 2007.

Speth, Gus. *America the Possible: Manifesto for a New Economy*. New Haven, CT: Yale University Press, 2013.

Stevens, Susan. *Nonprofit Lifecycles: Stage-Based Wisdom for Nonprofit Capacity*. Wayzata, MN: Stagewise Enterprises, 2001.

Wheatley, Margaret. *Leadership and the New Science: Learning About Organization from an Orderly Universe*. San Francisco: Berrett-Koehler Publishers, 1994.

Wiggins, Grant, and Jay McTighe. *Understanding by Design*. Expanded second edition published by Merrill Prentice Hall by arrangement with the Association for Supervision and Curriculum Development, Alexandria, VA. Upper Saddle River, NJ: Pearson Education, 2006.

INDEX

ABOUT THE AUTHOR

David Grant is the former president and CEO of the Geraldine R. Dodge Foundation in Morristown, New Jersey. He now consults with people and organizations that have a social or educational mission, specializing in strategic planning, design of assessment systems, and board development. During his years at the Dodge Foundation, Grant delivered over a hundred keynote addresses on a range of topics, led workshops titled

DOUG AUSTIN

"Measuring What Matters" for over two hundred nonprofit organizations, and received numerous awards.

Grant's career has centered on innovative teaching and learning. He has toured the world with his one-man show as Mark Twain. In 1983, he and his wife, Nancy Boyd Grant, co-founded the Mountain School of Milton Academy, a highly regarded, semester-long, interdisciplinary environmental studies program in Vermont for high school juniors from throughout the country. He has been a national consultant to schools and leader of workshops on topics of curriculum and program design, professional development, assessment practices, and school climate.

Grant has served as the town moderator of Vershire, Vermont, chair of the board of the Council of New Jersey Grantmakers, and a member of the board of directors of the Surdna Foundation in New York City. He is currently a trustee of three social profit (formerly called nonprofit) organizations.

He lives in Strafford, Vermont.

green press

INITIATIVE

Chelsea Green Publishing is committed to preserving ancient forests and natural resources. We elected to print this title on 100-percent postconsumer recycled paper, processed chlorine-free. As a result, for this printing, we have saved:

33 Trees (40' tall and 6-8" diameter)
15 Million BTUs of Total Energy
2,850 Pounds of Greenhouse Gases
15,454 Gallons of Wastewater
1,034 Pounds of Solid Waste

Chelsea Green Publishing made this paper choice because we and our printer, Thomson-Shore, Inc., are members of the Green Press Initiative, a nonprofit program dedicated to supporting authors, publishers, and suppliers in their efforts to reduce their use of fiber obtained from endangered forests. For more information, visit: www.greenpressinitiative.org.

Environmental impact estimates were made using the Environmental Defense Paper Calculator. For more information visit: www.papercalculator.org.

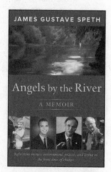